3 1000 00185801 1

W9-BUD-125

MOTIVATING TODAY'S EMPLOYEES

MOTIVATING TODAY'S EMPLOYEES

Lin Grensing-Pophal

Self-Counsel Press
(a division of)
International Self-Counsel Press Ltd.
USA   Canada

BELLEVILLE PUBLIC LIBRARY

Copyright © 1991, 2002 by International Self-Counsel Press Ltd.

All rights reserved.

No part of this book may be reproduced or transmitted in any form by any means — graphic, electronic, or mechanical — without permission in writing from the publisher, except by a reviewer who may quote brief passages in a review. Self-Counsel Press acknowledges the financial support of the Government of Canada through the Book Publishing Industry Development Program (BPIDP) for our publishing activities.

Printed in Canada.

First edition: 1991
Second edition: 2002

National Library of Canadian Cataloguing In Publication Data

Grensing-Pophal, Lin, 1959-
   Motivating today's employees

   (Self-counsel business series)
   Previously published as: Motivating today's work force.
   ISBN 1-55180-355-0

   1. Employee motivation. I. Grensing-Pophal, Lin, 1959-
Motivating today's work force. II. Title. III. Series.
HF5549.5.M63G742001   658.3'14   C2001-911265-3

Self-Counsel Press
(a division of)
International Self-Counsel Press Ltd.

1704 N. State Street
Bellingham, WA 98225
USA

1481 Charlotte Road
North Vancouver, BC V7J 1H1
Canada

CONTENTS

INTRODUCTION

In an economy with more people than jobs, employers tend not to worry a great deal about motivating their workers. But in an economy like that of the early 21st century, where skilled labor is scarce and jobs are plentiful, the ability to attract and retain qualified employees becomes extremely critical.

Employee turnover and the retention of valued employees were major problems in the late 20th century, according to a retention and staffing survey conducted by Manchester Partners International. The average turnover rate in the United States hovered at 15 percent. The costs associated with turnover can be high — generally 25 percent of the individual's annual salary. Aside from the obvious costs of advertising for, interviewing, and training replacement staff, there are more subtle costs, such as the impact of turnover on customer service and productivity.

Finding ways to attract and retain high-quality, front-line staff can be a boon to any business. The job market is competitive, the labor pool is shrinking, and employers are frequently vying for the same candidates. For small businesses, in particular, competing with larger employers can be difficult. Many small businesses can't afford to offer the level of salary or benefits that their larger competitors can easily provide. How then, can these small businesses hope to compete for talented employees?

By developing successful methods of motivating employees, even the smallest business can remain competitive. What does it take? As many companies are finding, it takes a commitment to making the workplace a rewarding one for staff members. It takes a solid understanding of employee needs and the willingness to do what it takes to meet those needs. It takes creativity and the willingness to move outside the restrictions of traditional benefits and rewards to embrace new methods of keeping employees active and energetic on the job.

It doesn't always take a lot of money, which can be good news to small businesses that struggle to meet their capital and expense needs while competing for qualified employees in a tight labor market.

As we'll find in a number of examples throughout this book, money is not the only way to motivate employees.

Consider, for example, the employees of Microsoft. Many of them have become millionaires because of their equity ownership in the company, yet they stay on the job. Why? Because Microsoft has a widely renowned casual and participative corporate culture that emphasizes both individual and team achievement. Money, quite obviously, is not everything.

The needs of employees have changed dramatically over the past 30 years. Fueled by a rapid increase in the number of women entering the workforce, more and more employees are expecting — and demanding — a balance between the expectations of work and the demands of personal life. No longer can managers tell employees to leave their personal lives at home. Today's managers must recognize that what happens at home has a dramatic impact on performance at work — and vice versa.

Today's workers value the opportunity to better balance work life and home life. Workers are most likely to be satisfied with their jobs, committed to their employers, and productive at work when they have jobs that offer autonomy, meaning, learning opportunities, support from supervisors, and flexible work arrangements that are responsive to individual needs, according to a comprehensive new study of the U.S. workforce released in 1998 by the Families and Work Institute and sponsored by KPMG.

Too often, managers feel that they know what their employees want. After all, most managers were once employees in similar positions themselves. But times change, perspectives change, and employee needs change. Sometimes it's the simple things that are overlooked.

Money, many businesses are finding, may not mean anything when it comes to retaining good employees. Motivation, however, is everything.

Part I

Part I:
The Basics
of Motivation

According to a 1998 survey by Watson Wyatt Worldwide, more than 9 out of 10 employers (92 percent) say that employees' level of job satisfaction is an "important" or "very important" factor in determining the number of lost work days. Survey results confirm what managers and employers have long known: the less satisfied employees are with their jobs, the more likely they are to miss work.

Why do employees come to work? For some, because they feel a sense of contribution — they enjoy their work. They believe they are making a difference, whether their job entails manufacturing parts, serving customers, or creating new products. For many, though, work is an obligation. Many employees come to work because they know they must. If they don't, they will be reprimanded and eventually terminated.

Which category of workers do you think is most likely to miss work from time to time — the workers who are there because they want to be, or the ones who are there because they feel they have to be?

The difference? Motivation.

1
MOTIVATIONAL THEORY

What motivates you? What does it take to make you want to spring from bed each morning to greet the new day? What does it take to make you feel excited and enthusiastic about tackling a new project? To make you want to commit to a goal, a project, or an organization?

Is it challenge? Recognition? Reward?

It may surprise you to know that it doesn't always take a grand gesture to make an employee feel motivated.

A woman who recently (barely!) survived a merger between two large energy companies says that what motivates her is "receiving a simple e-mail from a supervisor (or better yet, from someone higher than your supervisor) thanking you for a job well done. It's a very satisfying and positive item for a personnel file. It's also something that you can refer back to when you need a little reassurance that you are doing a good job."

A graphic designer says, "It's always fun when my boss brings around ice cream bars for those who are sticking it out late on one of those sunny Friday afternoons when spring fever has overtaken everyone else."

It may also surprise you that what motivates you doesn't necessarily motivate members of your staff.

One manager tells of an informal conversation between her and her staff members about motivating experiences. She shared with the group that one of the most motivating things to her was to receive a new assignment or challenge from her manager. A staff member spoke up and said, "Well, don't try to motivate me that way — I'd rather have a day off." Others chimed in: "I'd just like a note from you telling me I did a good job."

She was surprised: "You mean you're not motivated when I give you extra projects? I do that all the time."

"We know," they laughed. This group was fortunate to have had the opportunity to share this information so the manager could learn what her staff found motivating. Not all managers are so lucky.

What is motivation?

Motivation is a difficult term to define.

Merriam-Webster's Collegiate Dictionary doesn't offer much help:

Main Entry: mo.ti.va.tion

Date: 1873

1 : a : the act or process of motivating
    b : the condition of being motivated

2 : a motivating force, stimulus, or influence : INCENTIVE, DRIVE

Encarta's definition is better, particularly if we're thinking of motivation from a business standpoint:

Mo-ti-va-tion:

1. giving of a reason to act: the act of giving somebody a reason or incentive to do something

2. enthusiasm: a feeling of interest or enthusiasm that makes somebody want to do something, or something that causes such a feeling

3. reason: a reason for doing something or behaving in some way

4. PSYCHOLOGY forces determining behavior: the biological, emotional, cognitive, or social forces that activate and direct behavior

What do we, as managers, mean when we say we want to motivate our employees? Quite basically, we're saying that we want to "give them a reason or incentive to do something." That "something" is the act of performing certain tasks or duties that further the goals and direction of the organization.

How can we, as managers, generate "a feeling of interest or enthusiasm that makes somebody want to do something"?

What the theorists tell us about motivation

Business theorists have long speculated on how workers are encouraged to do more work in less time and be happy about doing it.

Frederick Herzberg

In the 1950s, industrial psychologist Frederick Herzberg found that certain job factors caused worker dissatisfaction and poor performance when they fell below a certain level. Yet these same factors failed to increase job performance once they reached an optimum level. He labeled these factors maintainers because they maintain a certain level of productivity. Maintainers include —

- ▶ salary,
- ▶ job security,
- ▶ company policies, and
- ▶ administration.

Once these factors reach an optimum level, merely providing more of them, according to Herzberg, will not produce an increase in productivity.

For example, consider the experience of a high-school student whose first job is as a front-counter clerk in a fast-food restaurant. The student is hired at minimum wage and is satisfied with the pay, company policies, and administration. The student is motivated to perform and is excited about the opportunity to earn money for the first time. That excitement lasts for the first several months on the job; the student performs well and even receives a pay increase after three months. But once the initial eager phase is over, the student starts to feel restless and a bit bored. It's not the money. It's not the policies or procedures. It's not the administration. What is it?

According to Herzberg's theory, the missing ingredient is motivators.

Herzberg identified several sources of job satisfaction, which he called motivators. Motivators include —

> ► achievement,

> ► recognition for achievement,

> ► the work itself,

> ► responsibility, and

> ► advancement.

Motivators make employees work harder. The more motivators there are, the harder an employee will work.

What sort of motivators might make this student work harder?

Achievement. This might involve learning new things or taking on new responsibilities.

Recognition for achievement. Recognition could entail pay increases, but it also includes less tangible forms of recognition, such as praise from management and colleagues, awards (certificates, plaques, an article about the employee in the organization's newsletter, etc.).

The work itself. A talented and enthusiastic high-school student will quickly learn the responsibilities of being a front-counter clerk in a fast-food restaurant. How could the work itself be changed to provide more variety or more challenge?

Responsibility. When an employee first starts with a company, he or she is not given a great deal of responsibility. The manager or supervisor may watch him or her closely for some time and be reluctant to allow the employee to take on responsibility and make decisions — even minor decisions. As the employee grows in the position, however, the opportunity for more responsibility — the ability to make independent decisions, to participate in special teams or task forces, or to initiate new projects — can provide motivation.

Advancement. For many employees, advancement can be a motivator. In this case, the front-counter clerk may be motivated by advancement to assistant supervisor of front-counter clerks, or some other position that is higher in the fast-food restaurant's hierarchy.

Herzberg's point is that maintainers merely maintain a behavior. More salary, more job security, better company policies or better administration may provide a certain level of satisfaction for the employee, but these maintainers will not generate "a feeling of interest or enthusiasm that makes somebody want to do something." Only motivators will do that.

Maslow's hierarchy of needs

Another early theorist, psychologist Abraham Maslow, developed what he called a need hierarchy, which classifies five levels of needs ranging from the concrete to the intangible. These needs are—

1) physiological comfort,

2) safety,

3) social fulfillment,

4) satisfaction of the ego, and

5) self-actualization.

Maslow believed that until an individual's basic needs (i.e., food and security) are satisfied, that individual will not be motivated by involvement in social activities, the opportunity to learn new things, or advancement. Only after each need in the hierarchy has been adequately met, according to Maslow's theory, would individuals be motivated to move on to higher-level needs.

For example, suppose you have recently employed a single mother who is struggling to care for three small children. She will initially be highly concerned with making enough money to meet her family's needs for food, shelter, and security. Money will be the driving factor in motivating this employee. Offering her the opportunity to serve on a special task force, or giving her additional responsibilities (unless those new responsibilities lead to a pay increase) will not be motivating to this individual.

However, suppose this woman begins to make enough money to provide adequately and appropriately for her family. The strong initial drive has been satisfied. At this point, the employee may be driven to pursue higher-level needs, such as establishing relationships with other employees, learning new tasks, or taking on more responsibilities. More money would, of course, be welcomed, but more money would not create the motivation to perform better, faster, or with more loyalty.

In reality, Maslow's theory doesn't work quite that simply. Each of the needs on the hierarchy are, to a certain degree, inter-related. While we strive to earn a good wage, we are also concerned with job stability, getting along with coworkers, being recognized for our achievements, and feeling some sense of intrinsic enjoyment of the work we do. In addition, the extent to which each of these needs is satisfied is continually shifting and changing as our life circumstances change. We may be making adequate wages and be quite satisfied with our incomes, but major life events (i.e., an illness in the family) may mean that our salaries are no longer adequate.

Maslow's hierarchy of needs can be instructive to a manager in that it points to the individual differences among employees and the need to recognize each individual's position on the hierarchy.

Motivating an employee who is well paid, well-liked, and highly satisfied with his or her job will be quite different from motivating an employee who does not make enough money to meet his or her basic needs, or an employee who is dealing with security issues in his or her personal life.

Theories X and Y

Strongly influenced by Maslow and his needs hierarchy, Douglas McGregor applied this hierarchy to the organizational structure. In the l960s, he came up with two opposing theories, which he called Theory X and Theory Y.

Theory X management stresses that human beings are essentially lazy and do not want to work. They need to receive direction and are motivated through the fear of punishment. In addition, Theory X proposes that the average employee tries to avoid responsibility and wants job security above all else.

Theory Y management states that people will use both self-control and self-direction. This theory suggests that the average employee learns not only to accept but also to seek responsibility.

Theory X organizations have a hierarchical structure and control employee behavior. Employees are treated as if they —

- ▶ are lazy and anxious to evade work whenever possible,
- ▶ need control and direction in order to perform well,
- ▶ have relatively little ambition, and
- ▶ avoid responsibility whenever possible.

Theory Y organizations function in an almost completely opposite manner. These organizations are characterized by integration. According to McGregor, integration involves "the creation of conditions such that the members of the organization can achieve their goals best by directing their efforts toward the success of the enterprise." Employees are treated as if they —

- ► enjoy physical and mental effort,
- ► direct themselves to meet objectives,
- ► relate achievement with certain rewards, and
- ► use a high degree of imagination, ingenuity, and creativity.

Many of the dotcom companies that became prevalent in the 1990s, though they began to fail financially, were successful in providing employment atmospheres that are strongly indicative of a Theory Y environment.

A seasoned businesswoman with more than 25 years of experience in a traditional business environment had this to say about her shift to a dotcom: "I can't believe how happy I have been in this particular position, and what a great creative environment it is. I actually enjoy getting up and coming to work every day."

Another former corporate employee says, "One of the exciting things about working in a dotcom are the intelligent, enthusiastic, energetic people that it attracts. The whole space buzzes with energy. Unfortunately, that hasn't always been the case in my personal experiences with some of the larger corporations I've been with."

Interestingly, what many dotcom employees point to as motivating in their new positions is their sense of contribution and the feeling that they are truly making a difference. Compare this to a comment from an employee for a publicly held corporation: "I had a manager who was very hands-off — so much so that if I went on vacation I'm sure he did not know I was gone. He never asked me how I was doing or if I needed any support from them unless it was review time. I finally transferred out of the department. I don't like a hovering manager, but I need to be recognized more than once a year."

Theory Z

Theory Z was advanced by William Ouchi and is often referred to as Japanese management style. The secret to success, according to Ouchi, is not technology but a special way of managing people. This management style involves a strong company philosophy, a distinct corporate culture, long-range staff development, and consensus decision making. The result is lower turnover, increased job commitment, and much higher productivity.

A major aspect of Theory Z is trust. Organizations spend a lot of time developing the interpersonal skills needed to make effective group decisions. When a group makes decisions, group members are asked to place their fate in the hands of others. Each person has responsibility for some individual objectives set by the group. Team performance is critical to the accomplishment of objectives.

Ouchi has said:

> *"Perhaps the single most notable characteristic among those who have succeeded at going from A to Z has been an almost palpable character of integrity. By integrity I do not mean preaching morality to others; I mean an integrated response to problems, an integrated and consistent response to customers and employees, to superiors and subordinates, to problems in finance and in manufacturing. A person of integrity treats secretaries and executives with equal respect and approaches subordinates with the same understanding and values that characterize his or her family relationships. A person with integrity can be counted upon to behave consistently, even as organizational conditions change. Such a person can be trusted and can provide that key human capital from which others can draw in the process of change."*

Applying the theories

Theories and classification systems are a good starting point for employers and managers looking for ways to improve employee performance, morale, and productivity. For real results, however, you need more than theory. You need a step-by-step, day-by-day, practical approach to motivating your employees so they will help your company run smoothly and profitably. How to motivate your employees without adding to the already high costs of your operations is the challenge that today's manager faces.

2

FACTS AND FALLACIES
ABOUT MOTIVATION

Are you motivated? How do you really know? Motivation can be a tough term to define — even when we relate the term to our own behavior. Imagine, then, how difficult it can be to spot, and reinforce, motivation in others.

But spot it we must if we wish to maintain a fully operational workforce. Employee turnover has risen to startling levels in the past two decades. According to a survey conducted by the Bureau of National Affairs, turnover increased from 1.1 percent per month in both 1997 and 1998 to 1.2 percent in 1999. Worse, turnover increased at an even greater pace for smaller companies (those with fewer than 250 employees) from .09 percent in 1998 to 1.2 percent in 1999.

There is no doubt that managers and business owners are critically aware of the need to motivate their staff members. Recruitment and retention are high on the list of corporate initiatives at most organizations as they struggle to maintain a fully functioning workforce. What it takes to keep employees on the job, however, is not necessarily clear to those attempting the task. In fact, a poll conducted of senior executives at Drake Beam Morin (DBM), a leading workplace consulting firm, revealed the following misconceptions about the impact of various practices on employee retention — misconceptions, says DBM, that organizations need to overcome.

1) "Show me the money." While there is no question that compensation is a very powerful lure to entice employees to accept new opportunities, money is not necessarily the answer to the retention issue. DBM's experience in working with people in career transition has found that career development and challenging work opportunities are often greater incentives than money to stay or start with an employer.

2) "Recruitment is a separate issue." Not so. An effective retention strategy begins at the earliest stages of the selection and recruitment process, according to DBM. Selecting the right people — those whose skill sets and attitudes fit the organization's needs and values — is critical to retention. Most turnover, they say, is due to "bad chemistry."

3) "Training will only make employees more marketable." In the long run, providing employees with the latest in learning opportunities may indeed raise their market value. However, it also helps to motivate them and enhance their performance in their current positions. Offering training and development opportunities is a very worthwhile retention strategy.

4) "We can't hold on to good people." The notion of holding on, which companies often use in a figurative sense, may mask a more literal problem, DBM says. The traditional view of retention, to which many companies still adhere, is the ability to hold on to or keep employees. Today's reality is that companies need to adopt a more flexible and understanding approach to meeting individual needs by creating an environment in which employees want to stay and grow. Employees need to be viewed as free agents, not fixed assets.

5) "Once they leave, who cares?" The traditional approach was to send departing employees on their way and not look back. However, valuable lessons may be learned from those who leave, most often during exit interviews, which can help bolster future retention rates.

Recruiting, retaining, and motivating employees is a complex process rife with misconceptions. Before going any further, let's take a closer look at some of most common myths surrounding the issue of motivation.

Fallacy #1: Motivation is the goal

As a manager, what do you want from your employees? Many managers might say, "I want them to be reliable, to come to work every day on time. I want them to be dependable; to produce consistent results. I want them to perform."

Is it enough to have "motivated" employees? No. Motivation should not be the end goal of your human resource activities. Motivation is not enough. Motivation must lead to something — and that something is the realization of your business goals and objectives.

It's not enough to have happy or satisfied employees. A team of happy employees may be highly motivated, but if their efforts are not being directed toward the accomplishment of specific business goals and objectives, what's the point?

The desire to motivate employees is driven by the need to operate a successful business. That may seem somewhat callous, but it is the reality of doing business. Even in a not-for-profit environment, there are certain goals and objectives that must be met — raising a certain amount of money to support the organization's mission, for example.

Suppose you have an administrative assistant who is extremely enthusiastic about her job. She comes to work every day, on time, ready to perform. But her dream is to be a graphic designer. The part of her job she loves the most is being creative with the documents she produces — she loves to find clipart on the Internet, and add it to memos and letters. She eagerly volunteers to create flyers for employee events and has developed a department newsletter on which she spends a great deal of time each week. Because she so enjoys these creative activities, she rushes through her other tasks. There is no doubt that your administrative assistant is a very motivated employee. But is she motivated to do the right things?

Yes, you should be concerned about motivating your employees. But you must recognize that motivation, in itself, is not the goal. The goal is the accomplishment of your business objectives — motivated employees are one of the tools that will allow your company to reach those objectives.

Fallacy #2: Money motivates

The idea that money is an effective motivator is perhaps the most common motivational myth. As Herzberg pointed out many years ago, money is a maintainer — not a motivator. Certainly pay is important and you need to ensure that employees are fairly paid in the context of both their coworkers and of the market in which you operate. But given a fair rate of pay, more money will not provide more motivation.

Good managers intuitively know that different things motivate different employees, says a Purdue University human resource expert, but putting a tailored plan into action is not as easy as it sounds. David Schoorman, who teaches human resource management at Purdue's Krannert School of Management, also consults extensively with industry. Schoorman says the structured "one-size-fits-all" corporate compensation plan can trip up even the most responsive, creative manager.

"A real challenge for supervisors and managers today is to figure out how to be that bridge between the standard benefit list of 'what you get' and what really motivates you as an employee," Schoorman says. "People putting together compensation and benefit plans often underestimate the value of growth opportunities, both professional and personal, as motivational tools."

Here's a very common example. An employee who has been doing an exceptional job, is paid well, and has been with your company for a number of years applies for a promotion to an open position. The position has also been advertised outside the company; in fact, a national search is under way to find the best applicant for the job. The internal applicant believes that he or she is that best applicant. Yet you find that external applicants offer broader experience, more varied backgrounds, and the fresh approaches you're hoping to inject into your company. You regretfully decide not to interview the internal applicant.

Over the next few months, this formerly motivated, highly energetic, and satisfied employee begins to exhibit signs of unrest. The employee is becoming withdrawn and uninvolved. The manager reports that the employee is taking more time off, refraining from putting in any extra effort, and is openly looking for work elsewhere.

Is it the employee's rate of pay that is causing the problem? No.

After considering the above example, you'll probably concede that, at best, money is a good sweetener. While it's a necessary aspect of any job, it's not enough to keep performance at a high level in the absence of other things — things like opportunities for advancement, recognition, involvement, and good communication. While a cake has to have sugar to make it taste good, it won't be a cake unless all the other ingredients are there. In the same way, in any job, money may make a position seem very attractive, but in the absence of other non-monetary aspects of a job, it won't be enough to keep an employee happy.

"In today's tight labor market, competitive pay is the price of admission for employers — it is not a key differentiator," says Rick Beal, a senior compensation consultant at Watson Wyatt and co-author of the firm's study *Strategic Rewards®: The New Employment Deals*. The study involved a survey of 551 large employers and over 500 employees. Only 15 percent of those surveyed said that expectation of financial reward had a very significant influence on performance. "Our research consistently shows that intangible factors such as personal satisfaction and recognition of contributions are more effective in driving high performance," says Beal.

Yes, you need to pay your employees, and pay them fairly, if you want a good job done. After a certain point, though — and this point will vary with each employee — money will no longer serve as an effective motivator. It is at this point that you'll need to turn to non-monetary incentives.

Fallacy #3: The Golden Rule applies

"Do unto others as you would have them do unto you." That's the golden rule and it's a rule that many of us have operated under for many years. The problem is, when it comes to motivating employees, it doesn't work.

Why not? Because the things that motivate you, as a manager, are very different from the things that motivate your employees. Managers are different from employees. They have different needs and drives. So while you may be extremely motivated when asked to lead a new project team, your employees may feel taken advantage of when given the same opportunity.

One manager tells of the insights she obtained after a department meeting in which she encouraged employees to share with her examples of what made them feel motivated. While her staff was motivated by recognition, hand-written notes, feedback on doing a good job, she was motivated by the opportunity to take on a new project or being assigned a new challenge. Guess how she was attempting to motivate her staff. Guess how well that was working!

The "platinum rule" is a better guide for managers: "Do unto others as they would have themselves done unto." In other words, find out what their needs and desires are and work to meet those needs and desires.

As this manager discovered, assuming that her staff members would be motivated by the same things that motivated her was inappropriate and could have, if gone unchecked, resulted in their alienation and frustration.

Fallacy #4: Motivators are universal

Motivators are not universal. One employee may be delighted that you care enough to remember his birthday and will improve his output 200 percent, while another employee may sneer when she's awarded the employee of the year award and may show no improvement in productivity.

Some employees simply want to do their jobs. They work at a fair but even pace. They are neither satisfied nor dissatisfied. They are not upwardly mobile.

Some employees need to be constantly prodded. Their managers are always trying to think of creative ways to provide incentives and boost productivity.

Some employees are easily motivated. They respond to almost any change in their environments, positive or negative.

Some employees are powerhouses of productivity. They are self-motivators. Their environments may seem free of any motivators, yet they consistently perform at or beyond their limits.

The point is, every employee is different. And, particularly in a business climate that is becoming increasingly diverse in terms of the age, ethnic background, beliefs, and desires of employees, it is becoming even more important to recognize that there is no such thing as a simple solution to the challenge of motivation. Each employee will respond uniquely to various motivators and incentives. The challenge to management is to identify the right motivators for each staff member — not always an easy task!

Fallacy #5: The burning platform can be a strong motivator

If all else fails, light a fire under 'em, and they'll get going, right? Not necessarily. While employees may rise to the occasion to help a failing company get over a financial hurdle, or compete against a fierce rival, burning platforms generally only lead to short-term motivation. When your financial problems continue quarter to quarter, or the competitor remains in town, threatening your existence, year after year, employees will lose their initial fire and resolve and resort to their old ways.

Behavioral psychologists have demonstrated for years that negative reinforcement is less effective as a means of changing behavior than positive reinforcement.

"Let's work hard so we can meet next quarter's financial goals and benefit from quarterly bonuses," will, therefore, be more motivating than, "Let's work hard so we can meet next quarter's financial goals and avoid pay cuts."

Certainly there are times when a burning platform truly exists, and you must quickly rally employees around a cause. That can be appropriate. Exercise caution, however, in resorting to this form of motivation too frequently.

Fallacy #6: Motivation doesn't matter as long as the job gets done

The old Theory X form of management can work. Employees can be prodded, bullied, and intimidated into performing. But for how long? Generally, only until a better job comes along. And the employees who aren't able to find better jobs are probably not the kind of employees you want on your payroll anyway.

A strong economy has forced many business owners and managers to take a more critical look at the way they recognize and reward their staff. The organizations that have only recently discovered the importance of motivating employees learned the hard way — and often after severe staffing issues — that motivation does matter.

Fallacy #7: In a poor economy, motivation doesn't matter

If our full-employment economy suddenly shifts to an employer's market, will motivating staff members become less important? Certainly not. Even in times when good employees were easy to find and the employment market was an employer's market, many companies recognized the importance of motivating their staff.

Motivation isn't only a recruitment and retention issue. It's a performance issue. Remember, motivation is a tool to generate high performance that will result in the accomplishment of the organization's objectives. Regardless of how well the economy is doing, what company doesn't want to perform at higher levels than expected?

Fallacy #8: Nobody's irreplaceable

Have you ever, after a valued employee gives his or her notice, said, "Oh well. Nobody's irreplaceable"? In some respects you may be right. Certainly if you try long enough, pay high enough, or are willing to settle for an employee who is merely good enough, you can replace anybody. You can fill the position, but can you fill the void?

The costs of replacing a staff member can be substantial, especially if you're replacing employees at top levels of the organization or employees who have very specialized skills.

A 1998 study by William M. Mercer Inc. indicated that 45 percent of the 206 medium-to-large U.S. companies polled reported that turnover cost them more than $10,000 per replaced employee. One-fifth of the respondents indicated that the cost was as high as $30,000 per employee.

Consider that the cost of turnover doesn't just include tangible costs of recruitment.

Some of the actual costs you'll have are the costs of advertising the new position, possibly the cost of a temporary employee to fill in until a new hire can be added to the staff, the cost of a recruitment agency, and perhaps the cost of travel and lodging for your candidates. But these costs do not represent the actual or only costs you'll experience.

Your actual costs go beyond the costs of recruitment and selection. They go beyond the costs of orientation and training. They include lost opportunity costs, and those costs can be difficult to measure.

Turnover costs also include a number of other intangible costs. For instance, consider the following:

- ▶ The prior investment made in the training and development provided to the employee while he or she was with your organization

- ▶ If the employee worked in a cost center, the cost of revenue lost while the position is being filled and while the new employee is getting acquainted with the business

- ▶ The cost of lost customers or clients who may follow the former employee to his or her new position

- ▶ The drop in productivity for other employees as they pick up the slack for the departing employee and the new hire until he or she becomes fully functional

- ▶ The cost of the supervisor's or manager's time in training and developing the new employee (an investment that could potentially be lost again if the new hire decides to leave your firm)

Consider, also, more global costs, such as the potential damage to your company's reputation if turnover becomes endemic and the classified ad section of the local newspaper continually carries ads for replacement positions. Think of the effect upon customer relations if customers must continually deal with new employees with whom they have not established relationships and who have not yet attained the level of expertise necessary to provide exceptional service.

If you've ever lost a valued employee and struggled to find and retrain a replacement, you know that some people truly are irreplaceable!

Fallacy #9: I can motivate my employees

Supervisors and managers certainly have a major impact on each employee's level of motivation and resulting productivity. But it takes a team — an entire organization — to provide the environment, the opportunities, and the framework for motivation to take place.

You cannot do it alone. You can, however, work with the other supervisors and managers in your organization, with the HR department, if your organization has one, and with upper management to recognize the importance of motivation and to implement the appropriate activities, practices, and culture to enhance the motivation of your staff.

Fallacy #10: Once a motivated employee, always a motivated employee

Motivation is not a destination; it's a state of mind and it can be fleeting. As an employer or manager, you will never reach a point where all of your employees are motivated and you can sit back and reap the rewards of your efforts. Some employees will be motivated some of the time. Through your efforts to establish a work environment that offers opportunity, reward, and recognition, you can work toward motivating more of your employees, more of the time. But that's about the best you can hope for.

The journey can be a satisfying and rewarding one. It can also be frustrating. There will be ups and downs. There will be failures. Your work team will sometimes be disgruntled. Individual members may leave.

Ultimately, though, you can have an impact. The impact is incremental and it can be transitory. But through persistence, vigilance, and a desire to build a staff of motivated individuals who work together to achieve the goals of the organization, you can make a difference.

3

WHAT MOTIVATES EMPLOYEES?

When Elaine was hired as a contract employee to do graphic design work for a small, privately held company, she looked forward to the opportunity to exhibit her creative skills. She didn't expect, though, that she would be welcomed into the firm and considered part of the family. As she says, "I was shocked when my supervisor invited me to attend a department meeting — I assumed temps weren't involved in those things. Then, at the meeting, I had the opportunity to give some pointers on a four-color process. That was motivating because I had the opportunity to show that I could contribute."

Another woman shares an experience that she felt was especially motivating: "Out of the blue one day, the owner of the company came by and gave me a $75 bonus for working on a project. I bought a freezer from another employee with the money."

Sue, a professional engineer, says that the most motivating thing to her is reporting to someone she respects — a mentor — and having that individual hand her new assignments. "I guess it conveys a level of trust," she says. She adds though, that new assignments aren't motivating if they come from individuals whom she doesn't respect. "When it's someone I look up to and whom I respect, it's flattering to be chosen for an assignment. In other cases, it just seems like more work. It's a subtle difference, I know, but it makes a difference to me."

"These things have never happened to me, but they would be motivating," says an employee who doesn't feel particularly motivated all of the time. "It would be great if my manager would say, 'Why don't you pick out a career-building seminar this year and we'll pick up the tab,' or if the company president would casually stop by just to say, 'Hey, thanks for your comment at the meeting today — you have some great ideas!' "

What motivates high performers? The answers may surprise you. It doesn't always take money. It doesn't always take grand gestures. Sometimes, as the not-so-motivated employee points out, all it takes is a simple pat on the back.

A study by Watson Wyatt of 551 large employers and more than 500 employees done in 2000 found that the majority of those responding — 81 percent — indicated that the "desire to maintain good work reputation" was "very significant" in terms of their motivation. Other motivations cited were "importance of the work" (76 percent), "appreciation of others" (66 percent), "interesting work" (51 percent), "personal desire to please supervisor" (20 percent), and "expectation of financial reward" (15 percent). Note that monetary reward was not the main driver that we often believe it to be.

Motivators for the 21st century

As the labor market continues to tighten, innovative companies are reaching deeper and deeper into their bag of incentives to recruit, retain and motivate employees. Interestingly, it is not the offer of higher salaries or stock options that encourages most workers. In fact, one of the most desired benefits for many workers is work/life balance, according to a 2000 study by Wirthlin Worldwide, which was commissioned by Xylo, a company that helps clients motivate employees through the establishment of work/life programs.

In the survey of 1002 workers, 71 percent cited reasons other than salary and bonuses as factors that influence their job satisfaction and motivation. Four factors stood out when employees were asked to indicate what caused them to feel satisfied or motivated on the job:

> ▶ 29 percent said additional perks, benefits, and employee discounts

- 25 percent said a good salary and bonuses

- 23 percent said a work environment that is fun and enjoyable

- 22 percent said recognition and respect for work performance

The results of this study are consistent with what other researchers have found. According to another study by the Radcliffe Public Policy Center in Cambridge, Massachusetts, white-collar workers value time more than money. This is especially true in workers between the ages of 20 and 39. Family time topped the list of workplace priorities for 82 percent of men and 85 percent of women aged 20 to 39 in the study.

Results of these studies aside, however, it's important to keep in mind that no two people are the same. No two of your employees are the same. Consequently, no single motivator is going to work with all of your employees. Some employees — and often these are lower-level employees — will be positively influenced by money. Others — those with family commitments — may be motivated by time off or flexible work scheduling. Still others may crave independence and the ability to be involved in decision-making. To motivate effectively, you need to know more than what the motivators are. You need to know which motivators will work with which people.

The needs and values of today's workforce are very different from the needs and values of the workforce 50 years ago — or even ten years ago. Today's workers are better educated, less interested in following orders, more loyal to themselves than to the company, and more concerned about meeting their own needs.

Furthermore, today's employees are impatient. They are not willing to wait years for a pay increase, a promotion, or new opportunities. They will not bide their time in an organization if they do not feel they are being valued or given the opportunities and benefits they demand.

This presents a major challenge for employers and managers. The current generation of workers can be very difficult to motivate. According to the Bureau of Labor Statistics, the number of people working or looking for work is projected to increase by 17 million between 1998 and 2008, reaching 155 million. This growth will be affected by the aging of the baby-boom generation (those born between 1946 and 1964). At the same time, the number of persons in the labor force between the ages of 25 and 44 is projected to decrease.

As these dramatic shifts are taking place, the number of management jobs will fall sharply. Promotions may not be available.

What happens when an employee works at the same job, year after year, with no chance for promotion? He or she becomes dissatisfied and, eventually, non-productive. To maintain job satisfaction under these circumstances, employers must come up with creative ideas for employee motivation. To do this, they must first determine what motivates their employees.

What employees want

Many employers assume they know what their workers want and believe they are providing it. For example, they may point to good wage and benefit packages as proof that they are doing well by their employees. But sometimes, when we think we know what motivates our workforce, we may be wrong.

Sue Marczinke has been with Royal Credit Union (RCU) in Eau Claire, Wisconsin, for more than twenty years. Marczinke started at RCU through a cooperative education program sponsored by her high school. "I started out doing microfilming, receipts, and things like that. I did some receptionist work in the lobby — answered phones and greeted people." Later she went to vocational school to pursue a degree in accounting, all the while remaining at RCU. She worked in the accounting department for about two years, in customer service for about 14 years, and was recently promoted to a position in the employee services and development department.

What has kept her with RCU all of these years? "I would say the employees that I worked with," Marczinke says, "I always had really good staff that I worked with. I always felt very stable. I never felt threatened that RCU was not going to be there. I always had good supervision — I think that's important. If you have a good supervisor that you can trust and that helps you, I think that makes a big difference, and I was lucky enough to have that."

You may notice that money wasn't at the top of the list for Marczinke. In fact, when asked about the impact of pay, Marczinke says, "I always felt the pay was fair for what I was doing."

Employee commitment

Unfortunately, Marczinke's attitude is fast becoming a rare phenomenon. A study by Watson Wyatt Worldwide, the WorkCanada™ survey, conducted during the summer of 1999, polled more than 1,600 Canadian employees at all job levels and across many industries about their attitudes toward their workplaces and their employers. The results of the study indicate that employee commitment in the Canadian workplace is on the decline. Of those surveyed, only 49 percent indicated that they are committed to their employers, establishing the lowest level of employee commitment in the firm's four surveys conducted over the past ten years. In 1991, the level of commitment was at 62 percent, but has fallen steadily since. At 49 percent, the Canadian level of commitment is 6 percent less than that reported by American workers in a similar survey.

In addition, 57 percent said they were not positive about their company leaders, only 52 percent were satisfied with their supervisors, and 60 percent were dissatisfied with their input into hiring and evaluation decisions.

The survey showed that five key factors drive employee commitment, with employer awareness of people issues topping the list. These issues involve: recruiting and retention procedures, valuing diversity, providing job security for good work, recognizing the need to balance work and family responsibilities, providing flexible working arrangements, and preparing people to work in a changing environment. Other key drivers of commitment in the Canadian study were —

- ► job environment,
- ► communicating business goals, strategies, and results,
- ► compensation satisfaction, and
- ► management performance.

The U.S. study identified seven key factors. In order of importance, they are —

- ► trust in senior leadership,
- ► chance to use skills on the job,
- ► job security,
- ► competitiveness of rewards,
- ► quality of company's products/services,
- ► absence of work-related stress, and
- ► honesty and integrity of company's business conduct.

Notably, the study showed variation between responses from Canadian and U.S. workers, in addition to responses from different sectors of the workplace and different levels of employees within the organizations. Employees in the high-tech sector reported higher levels of commitment than those in financial services or manufacturing. Healthcare workers demonstrated the lowest level of commitment. Commitment was also found to be related to the employee's position in the organization — fewer workers and supervisors were as committed as managers and executives.

Why is commitment important? Watson Wyatt has determined that companies with highly committed employees had a 112 percent three-year total return to shareholders, compared to a 76 percent return for companies that exhibited low employee commitment. Clearly, commitment makes a difference.

Generating commitment among employees through motivation can be a daunting task. As we've seen, employees do not respond collectively to an employer's practices or a supervisor or manager's efforts; employees respond individually.

Employee retention

Joan Stewart, author of the booklets *113 Tips for Recruiting Valuable Employees* and *107 Tips for Keeping Valuable Employees* (www.publicityhound.com/tips.html) says companies are responding to employee needs in a variety of ways. These include —

- ► flexible work schedules so people can take care of kids and elderly parents,
- ► mandatory paid sabbaticals that must be taken aside from regular vacations,
- ► advertising themselves as "gay-friendly" workplaces to attract gay job applicants during this difficult labor shortage,
- ► offering more and better training that contributes to the employees' career goals,
- ► offering closer contact with executives at the top through things such as "Breakfast with the Boss" programs, and
- ► doing quarterly performance reviews instead of annual reviews.

Today's tight labor market and increased desire for work/life balance is leading to employees demanding — and receiving — more unusual recruitment perks such as portable vacation time, outsourcing laundry services, and providing child and elderly care, says Drake Beam Morin (DBM), a global workplace consulting firm.

How can you find out what it will take to retain the front-line workers at your organization? The answer may seem simplistic — and it is simple. Ask them. What might asking them entail? With a small company, it could be as simple as talking to employees — and listening. (See chapter 6 for a discussion on communication.)

With larger groups of employees, or to get more quantitative results, employee surveys can prove useful. Employee satisfaction surveys can help uncover issues that need to be addressed before it's too late. They can help management avoid losing a good employee because of an issue that could have been remedied. Another benefit is that employee surveys can indirectly communicate to employees that management is concerned about making the workplace a better working environment.

Finding out what your employees want

Do you really know what your employees want? To determine just how much your perception of what your employees want differs from what they really want, complete Sample 1 and, without revealing your rankings, ask your employees to complete the same form.

"There's a huge gap between what managers think employees want and what they really want," says a credit union executive. "It seems as though the employees we hire these days aren't looking for security in long-term careers, whereas the managers have already decided this is the path they want to take. They don't understand that everybody doesn't think the same way. I've been here for 22 years and I can't imagine working anywhere else, so for me it's hard to understand how a young person coming in doesn't see it in a long-term perspective."

The differences in the way you rank different aspects of employment may surprise you. Don't assume you know what your employees want. They may not be like you — in fact, they probably aren't like you. Take the time to discover what your employees really want.

Sample 1

WHAT DO EMPLOYEES REALLY WANT?

Rank from 1 to 10 (10 being highest) what you think employees want from their jobs. Circulate the same list to your employees (without your rankings), asking them to fill out the form based on their actual needs and wants.

Where are the gaps between your ratings and their ratings?

FACTOR	YOUR RANK	EMPLOYEE RANK
Understanding of personal issues		
Interesting work		
High wages		
Job security		
Loyalty of supervisor		
Tactful discipline		
Full appreciation of work done		
Feeling of belonging		
Good working conditions		
Opportunity for promotion		
The ability to learn new things		

How can you determine what motivates your employees?

1) Ask them. Go to each of your employees and ask them what things they like most (and least) about their jobs. Ask them specifically, "What are some of the things that the company does to increase your self-esteem?" "What are some of the things that the company does to decrease your self-esteem?" Their answers will give you the starting point you need to develop some effective ways of motivating them.

2) Find out what your employees do in their spare time — both at work and at home. Observe them during break periods and lunch hours. Do they spend their time relaxing? Socializing? Reading? Working?

3) Consider past experiences. To what has the employee responded favorably in the past? What type of projects or assignments really create a high level of productivity? What types of assignments create apathy?

It seems so easy, yet far too many managers and small-business owners fail to take this very important step. Don't make the mistake of transferring your own likes, dislikes, and desires to employees. The simplest way to find out what motivates your employees is to talk to them. Another way is to observe them. Knowing the interests of your employees when they are away from work is as helpful as knowing their interests on the job.

Putting it all together

Once you've listened to your employees comments and observed their actions, how can you put this new information into motivational practice?

First consider the maintainers: pay and benefits. You need to make sure that your pay and benefits package is equitable internally and competitive externally. These basics do matter. But today, companies also need to look beyond the basics at some less typical considerations, like non-traditional benefits. Do you have flextime? Do you have PTO (paid time off) days, rather than the traditional vacation days? Is your technology up to date? Even things like whether employees' office furniture is in good shape, or how clean the breakroom and restrooms are can make a difference.

Next, consider how well you keep employees informed and involved. Today's employees have a hunger to learn and to grow. They want to be involved — and they have a lot to offer.

Front-line managers have a critical impact on employee relations in any organization. Managers are the first point of contact for employees and have a very strong influence on employees' job satisfaction, morale, and motivation. Management can impact employees at many stages in the employee life cycle and in many ways. Managers are responsible for a great many tasks and topics, including hiring, conveying job requirements, communicating, training, and redirecting, or, in some cases, reprimanding employees. These issues will be discussed in detail in later chapters.

Organizations can't afford to ignore employee relations issues that can have a negative impact on recruitment, retention, and motivation. Have a look at Sample 2 to help you determine whether your company is in danger of losing unmotivated, yet important, staff.

Make sure that your employees know what is expected of them; provide them with the tools and resources to do the job, and act quickly to correct behaviors or performances that don't support the organization's goals or philosophies. The best way to keep employees motivated is to keep them involved.

Sample 2

Caela Farren, President of MasteryWorks, Inc. (www.masteryworks.com), in Annandale, Va., and an expert on organization career development and management, says that managers who cannot answer "yes" to the following important questions are at an increased risk of losing employees. Thinking of one of your key staff people, answer the following questions:

1. Do you know why this person works for the company and not somewhere else?

2. Have you talked with this employee about several career options and does he or she feel he or she is moving in that direction?

3. Do you know this person's number-one career concern and are you working with him or her to address it?

4. Do you know how valuable this person's skills are in the competitive market?

5. Do you remain vigilant for any sign of fatigue or overwork and do you take prompt supportive action to correct it?

6. Do you have an open, trusting, respectful relationship with this person?

7. Does this employee know that he or she is fairly compensated for his or her contributions?

8. Do you know what the employee's long-term goals are and are you actively supporting him or her?

9. Does this person's work environment meet his or her personal and professional needs?

10. Has this person's mood, physical health, and overall disposition been stable in the past six months?

11. Does this employee's values fit the corporate culture?

12. Is this person's profession and expertise critical to the organization?

13. Does this person have enthusiasm and passion for the work he or she is doing?

14. Does this employee seem satisfied with his or her work situation — projects, colleagues, reputation, and learning opportunities?

15. Does this employee know you will actively promote his or her development via training, challenging projects, and learning opportunities?

Part II

Part II:
The First Line of Influence

"True leadership skills are hard to come by," says an employee who is frustrated with the promotion practices of the company she works for. "Many times, a promotion has killed working relationships because the person promoted has not been at least introduced to real leadership skills. Not very motivating to either party."

Managers have a supremely critical impact on the satisfaction of an organization's workers but, as this employee points out, managers are often not provided with the education, training, coaching, and mentoring needed to succeed in these critical roles. The result? Disgruntled and unmotivated employees.

Research conducted jointly by Hay/McBer and Harvard University in 2000 confirms that the team leader is central to team success. The findings confirmed that leaders of outstanding teams share the following traits and approaches. Effective team leaders —

> ▶ *Lead real teams.* They know who the members of the team are, they have a plan, and they hold themselves jointly accountable for a collective task.

- *Are not necessarily charismatic leaders.* Effective leaders leverage the talent of their people to drive success. What does this mean for organizations? It means that charismatic employees should not always be promoted to managerial roles based on the assumption that they will be strong leaders.

- *Have unique characteristics.* They rely on leadership styles that promote dialogue and discussion. They are not authoritarian or coercive.

- *Focus on what really matters.* According to the Hay Group, there are five key conditions that make the greatest difference to performance:

    i.   Articulating a clear and compelling direction for the team.

    ii. Establishing a structure that helps the team do its work.

    iii. Selecting the best people for the team — and keeping them motivated.

    iv. Providing ongoing organizational support

    v.   Providing expert coaching

- *Understand that only they can be responsible for establishing clear direction and ensuring that team norms are maintained.* These tasks can not be delegated or shared.

- *Are more "emotionally intelligent."* Members of outstanding teams, according to the study's authors, "show the qualities of interpersonal sensitivity and integrity."

It all starts at the top. As a supervisor or manager, you lay the foundation for motivation in your work group. Through your words, your actions, and your deeds, you have a marked impact on your work group.

Laying the foundation means that you can effectively perform all of the key managerial functions: recruitment and selection, teambuilding, training, leading, motivating, controlling, coaching, counseling, evaluating, disciplining, and, sometimes, terminating.

While the organization certainly has an impact on employee morale through its programs and policies, you as a manager or supervisor have direct responsibility for, and direct impact on, the employees you manage. You also have the ability to provide input to your superiors to help them design programs, practices, and policies that will have a positive impact on employee motivation.

The third section of this book will focus on organizational initiatives that can impact motivation; this section focuses on the role of the front-line manager.

You are a front-line manager whether you are the owner of the company, the CEO, a vice president, a manager, a director, or a supervisor. In each of these roles, you will have direct responsibility for at least one individual who reports to you. In each of these roles, you are the first line of influence.

This is an critical role. To be successful you have to want to succeed. You have to understand that you have a tremendous impact on the effectiveness of your employees. And you have to believe that each of your employees is an important part of your overall work team, whether you're directing a team of two or a team of two thousand.

4

FINDING
THE RIGHT FIT

Hiring is where it all begins, and choosing an employee from a pool of candidates is one of the most important decisions that you, as a manager, will make. The right choice can positively impact the organization's culture, service, and bottom line. The wrong choice can lead to the excessive turnover, absenteeism, dissatisfaction, and low morale that contribute to low productivity.

Job seekers are continually on the move, with nearly four out of 10 U.S. workers seeking new job opportunities in 2001, according to a national Job Satisfaction Survey from Career Builder, an online career network. Although generally satisfied with their jobs, the survey indicated that more workers planned to change jobs in 2001 than in 2000.

"There's a new breed of worker — the silent job seeker — who is constantly on the lookout for new opportunities and who remains optimistic, even with the recent news of layoffs and restructurings," said Diane Strahan, a career expert with Career Builder. "Don't confuse their silence and satisfaction with job complacency," she warns.

What are these employees looking for? Better salaries, good job location, and great work/life balance all rated among the most important factors when considering potential job opportunities, according to the survey.

Employee absenteeism, according to a Watson Wyatt's 2000 Canadian Staying@Work survey, is also having a greater impact on the bottom line than ever before. Direct disability and absence-management costs represent 7.1 percent of payroll, up from 5.6 percent in 1997. According to the survey:

- ▶ Short-term absence costs, as a percentage of total payroll costs, have more than doubled from 2.0 percent in 1997 to 4.2 percent.

- ▶ Long-term disability costs, as a percentage of total payroll costs, have increased by 8 percent since 1997.

- ▶ The average direct cost of employee absenteeism in Canada is now $3,550 per employee per year.

- ▶ Direct and indirect costs combined — including costs for replacement workers such as lost productivity — account for 17 percent of payroll.

In addition to these tangible costs, having the wrong employee in the wrong job can lead to a multitude of less tangible problems. There is no question that making the right hiring decisions is critical to long-term effectiveness in building a motivated and productive staff. It can be challenging and intimidating to face the prospect of hiring a new employee, or replacing an employee who is leaving the organization. In fact, it should be a little intimidating. The addition of a new person to your work team is a very important decision.

Attracting employees is a challenge that every company faces. Surprisingly, according to a survey by CareerBuilder and POWER Hiring, Inc., a training and consulting organization, what employers think employees want (and what they include in their job advertisements) doesn't always mesh with what today's employees are really looking for. The survey suggests that employers may be too focused on big-picture issues while job seekers want to know how the job will impact their day-to-day lives.

For example, employers were most likely to rank company vision (35 percent) and job responsibilities (34 percent) as the most important elements of a job ad. While a large number of candidates rank job descriptions as most essential (28 percent), a large number also care a great deal about compensation (25 percent) and required job skills and education (20 percent). Only 8 percent of job seekers surveyed ranked company vision as most essential.

The poll also uncovered other gaps between job seekers and employers. When choosing between two positions with identical salaries, job seekers (28 percent) were most likely to rank job locations and telecommuting options as the most important determining factors, while employers felt that corporate culture and quality of coworkers (36 percent) were benefits they would promote to encourage candidates.

Both groups agreed that employee testimonials are the best way to evaluate potential companies (chosen by 52 percent of job seekers and 39 percent of employers).

"Top candidates are most interested in what they will be doing on the job," says Lou Adler, president of POWER Hiring. "We recommend to employers that 50 percent of any job advertisement should focus on what the candidate needs to accomplish. Add to that a compelling growth path and a little information on the corporate environment and you've created a compelling opportunity."

Hire right

Before you can even think of hiring somebody for a new or existing position, you have to know what you're looking for both in terms of technical and social/cultural skills. In fact, more and more managers and employers are coming to realize that it's not only competency that counts. It's attitude. It's personality. It's the ability to fit in with the workgroup.

The sports arena provides some good examples of how even the most highly skilled players and coaches may not prove to be a good fit for their team. Consider the experiences of Dennis Rodham or Bobby Knight.

Peter Salovey of Yale University and John Mayer of the University of New Hampshire coined the term "emotional intelligence," or EQ, a concept which became popular with the general public when Daniel Goleman's book, *Emotional Intelligence — Why It Can Matter More Than IQ*, hit the best-seller list.

Emotional intelligence is popularly defined as a set of skills, attitudes, abilities and competencies that determine an individual's behavior, reactions, state of mind and communication style. Goleman says that an individual's success at work is 80 percent dependent on EQ and only 20 percent dependent on IQ.

When employers talk about emotional intelligence, what they're really talking about is employee behavior. Does the behavior exhibited by the employee match the demands of the job? Whether we call it emotional intelligence or simply maturity, what we're really talking about is *fit* — we want to hire individuals for positions in which they will be most effective, technically and interpersonally. The concept of fit is critical in developing a productive work team.

Determining fit can be difficult. It requires a combination of quantitative and qualitative assessments of job skills, emotional maturity, and personality. It also requires that you match those skills to the mission and culture of the organization.

One tool that has been designed to help organizations consider candidate fit is the Predictive Index (PI), which was developed by Arnold S. Daniels. The test consists of some 86 adjectives on each side of a single sheet of paper. Side one asks test takers to check those words they feel describe the way others expect them to act; side two asks them to check the words they believe really describe them (in a work setting). The test takes about 10 to 15 minutes to complete.

Lens Express, a company that sells contact lenses and other eye wear, used the Predictive Index in a study of their telephone representatives to better understand the type of individual most suited to the requirements of the job.

"We needed to find people who could sell but who were interested in more than just a one-time sale," said Terri Lavertu, Manager of Human Resources. "We wanted employees who would work well in a team approach to selling and customer service and who would stay with the company. Using PI, Lens Express identified the individuals who would be successful selling their products over the phone as well as what it would take to keep them productively employed at the company. The company found that aggressive, high-powered sales people who were successful in other companies did not have enough freedom or flexibility in the jobs at Lens Express. Nor did they have the attention to detail needed to ensure that customers were always satisfied.

Using the test information, the company is now able to identify and hire people who will work within the Lens Express structure to deliver products and work with others on their team to reach sales goals. Employee retention was improved by 35 percent.

What do you consider when filling a position in your company? Do you look at the job skills, experience, and education of each candidate? Do you look any further than this? The concept of fit relates to each organization's unique culture. Organizations have personalities just like people do. Not all employees will easily fit into each culture — even if the employee's background and education are perfect for the position.

Suppose that one of your organizational values is collaboration. When you are interviewing an individual for a position, you would want to consider whether the applicant can consider the views of others when trying to reach a conclusion or accomplish a task. Another value might be teamwork. As you interview candidates, you would attempt to draw out from the applicant whether he or she prefers to work independently or as part of a team.

Obviously, the right fit will vary from one company to another. Identifying, defining, and pinning down what your company means by fit can be challenging. But, if done effectively, it can serve as the basis for building a strong and productive organization.

W.L. Gore, for instance, has a strong organizational culture that extends back to the company's beginnings more than 40 years ago. The culture is based on four core values that were initially crafted by company founder, Bill Gore. These core values continue to play an important role when selecting associates (Gore's employees are referred to as associates) today.

A good way to get started on determining what key traits your company values in employees is considering the traits and characteristics of your best performers. If you can define the indicators for success in people whose skills you value, you can start to develop some criteria by which to judge other candidates.

When hiring based on fit, you must be able to specifically identify why this strategy is important to your company, what traits and characteristics you can objectively tie to employee success, how to judge job applicants based on these traits, and be ready to nurture the continued expression of those characteristics through training, evaluation, promotion, and termination decisions.

There are some risks involved, however, in being too focused on fit. Prime among these is the risk of building a workgroup that is too similar and, consequently, too likely to suffer from what Irving Janis, in the 1970s, identified as "group think." According to Janis, some groups had such a high level of conformity that their ability to critically evaluate ideas was hampered. Group think wasn't eradicated in the 1970s, despite Janis' warnings. The same tendency exists today and may be furthered by a growing trend in organizations to hire individuals who closely match an existing corporate culture.

Certainly it's important for employees to share a core set of values, and it is appropriate to hire people based on their demonstration of those values. Still, organizations must exercise caution. In a rapidly changing business, technical and social environment, you don't want to build an organization that is so homogeneous that there is no one willing to suggest a change in direction, no one willing to stray from the status quo, no one willing to shout, "Hey, the emperor isn't wearing any clothes!"

Be cautious, too, in the use of personality tests when making hiring decisions. According to a poll created by CareerBuilder Inc., one fourth of job seekers are either reluctant to take employer-mandated personality tests or would refuse to take such tests — 12 percent would end the interview immediately, 6 percent would refuse the test, but would want to continue the interview, and 8 percent would take the test reluctantly.

When using these tests, says Rob McGovern, chairman and CEO of Career Builder, "it's important that they are job-seeker friendly and not overly lengthy, and that time is spent communicating with the applicant throughout the process."

In spite of the potential problems and detractors, most agree that hiring based on cultural fit is a legitimate business goal, as long as the company finds an acceptable balance — both legally and practically — in terms of avoiding inadvertent under-utilization of various types of employees and ensuring that the profile isn't so restrictive that it hinders the influx of new ideas and perspectives.

Your goal when filling any position is to find the best person for the job. By definition, the best person is the one who most closely meets the qualifications for the position. Qualifications refer to objective characteristics of the job applicant — not personal characteristics (like sex, age, race, etc.). To avoid falling victim to unintentional bias, you should be careful to —

- ➤ specifically identify the knowledge, skills, and abilities needed to do the job, and

- ➤ measure all candidates — objectively — against the criteria you've established.

Measuring emotional intelligence can be part of this process. If a position requires tact and diplomacy when dealing with external customers, for example, this might become part of the selection criteria. The point, though, is to clearly identify those traits — both technical and interpersonal — against which you will be judging all candidates.

Managers can get into trouble when they let personal opinions and biases interfere with hiring decisions. "I don't feel comfortable working with women." "Older employees are stubborn and will be difficult to manage." At best, these stereotypes can lead you to overlook a qualified candidate. At worst, they can land you in court.

To avoid trouble, be objective and realistic about the qualifications needed for the job. Some of the questions you should ask yourself include the following:

- ➤ What is the primary purpose of the job?

- ➤ What are the difficulties of the job?

- ➤ How much supervision is provided?

- ➤ What types of people must the new employee get along with?

- ➤ What technical knowledge or experience is required?

Consider these two key points when hiring:

1) Involve a broad cross section of people in the hiring process. This isn't a decision you want to make on your own. The new hire will need to interact effectively with numerous people within your company, and it makes sense to involve at least some of those people in the hiring process. If nothing else, it will give you a means of measuring your own perceptions. More important, it ensures that the candidate you select will be a good fit.

2) Make sure you give employees an accurate description of what the job really entails. As a manager, you're understandably eager to fill open positions and, particularly in a high-employment environment, it can take a lot of time to do so. However, it's a mistake to mislead an employee or make the job sound better than it is in order to land a key candidate.

Start employees off on the right foot

While you may breath a sigh of relief once you've selected a candidate for an open position and the candidate has accepted your offer, your job is far from over. In fact, it's just beginning. Those first few days and weeks in a new job — whether the employee is transferring from within the company, or is new to the organization — are key to a long-term positive relationship. Taking the time to start this new relationship off on the right foot is critical. Managers are busy — no doubt about it. But you need to make the time to get ready for the new hire and to ensure that he or she is appropriately oriented to the position, the work team, and the company.

The first step is notifying internal staff about the new hire. Be positive. Build the new candidate up. Focus on the traits the candidate will bring to the position that point to future success. You are managing the expectations of other team members during this process and want to alleviate any concerns that may exist about the candidate being inexperienced or under-qualified, or simply foreign to the company's corporate culture. While this initial introduction can take place over e-mail or through a memo, you will also want to identify key individuals in the company who should be scheduled to meet face to face with the new employee soon after he or she begins.

If the new employee will be working with specific customers outside the organization, take the time to notify these people as well. And, depending on the level and visibility of the position, you may also wish to send a news release to area media.

Just as in the interview, you will come to the orientation session with certain expectations. You will expect to provide the employee with pertinent information about the company and its policies, determine the extent of the employee's training and experience as it relates to specific job duties, develop feelings of belonging and acceptance and avoid creating unnecessary anxiety. During the orientation period you also want to provide the employee with copies of the job description, job specifications, and job standards.

As in virtually every aspect of human relations, you and your new employee will differ somewhat in what you expect the orientation and initial training period to accomplish. This is a natural dichotomy. Each of you will come to this initial meeting with different hopes and fears. The employee, of course, hopes to do a good job. But the employee has another, perhaps even more important, expectation — that he or she will fit in by getting along well with supervisors and co-workers.

As an employer, your major hope is that the employee will succeed and, in essence, make you look good. After all, you were the person responsible for hiring and you are now the person responsible for training. You can see, then, that while training the employee to do a good job is going to be important, your first goal should be to make the new employee feel comfortable by establishing a sense of belonging.

What can you do to make the orientation session successfully meet your training needs while minimizing anxiety for the employee? Following are some guidelines that may prove helpful.

Welcome

First you should welcome the employee and reestablish the rapport that you had during your initial interview. Begin with some small talk and move slowly into the real business of the meeting. Acknowledge the fact that the employee may be uncomfortable and nervous, and demonstrate your acceptance of these feelings. Once you sense that your new employee is becoming more relaxed, you're ready to move into the information session that begins the orientation session.

Organization chart

It's important that the new employee understands the structure of the company and how his or her position fits into that structure. At the beginning of the orientation session, you will want to show the new employee a copy of the organizational chart and explain how the departments and divisions are organized and how the new employee's department relates to others in the company. This is also the time to explain the chain of command in your organization.

Company and department objectives

What are the goals of the company? The new employee will need to know the answer to this question to be able to understand how he or she can contribute to these objectives. This broad question can be broken down as follows:

- ▶ What is the reason for the company's existence?
- ▶ What product or service is provided?
- ▶ What is the history of the organization?
- ▶ What is the company philosophy?
- ▶ How does the department in which the new employee will work contribute to the objectives of the company?

The new employee will have to know the answers to all of these questions to be able to understand how he or she fits in.

Working conditions

Much of what you will want to cover in terms of working conditions should be included in the employee handbook. Don't make light of this area, however. Surprisingly enough, the majority of new employees are more anxious, initially, about such things as where to eat lunch and where to park than they are about their job descriptions. By clearing up some of these questions and making sure that the employee is comfortable with the house-keeping aspects of the job, you will be able to move on to areas that deal more directly with job performance.

You will want to let your new employee know about such things as —

- ▶ hours of work and opportunities for flexible scheduling;
- ▶ lunch hours;
- ▶ coffee breaks;
- ▶ location of lunchroom or cafeteria;
- ▶ location of restrooms;
- ▶ company policy on personal phone calls and mail;
- ▶ payday — how often, how much, and how to keep track of this very important aspect of employment;

- ► special company functions and amenities such as the summer picnic, holiday party, or recognition of employees' birthdays;

- ► dress code; and

- ► how co-workers and supervisors should be addressed (by Mr. and Ms. or on a first name basis).

You will be surprised at how much more relaxed your new employee will be once some of these social issues are explained. And be sure to offer plenty of opportunity for questions — there may be something you've neglected to cover that the employee considers important.

Job responsibilities and job standards

At this point in the orientation session, you should provide the new employee with a copy of the job description for the position and go over it, point by point, so that every aspect of the job responsibilities and requirements will be fully understood. You also want to let the employee know what the job standards are. What level of performance do you expect? How, and when, will the employee be evaluated? Be very clear about your expectations now so you can avoid problems later.

Company standards

You will need to provide the new employee with information on company rules and procedures. What sort of behavior do you expect from employees? How flexible is the company in terms of working hours and personal time? What are the disciplinary procedures? On what basis would a termination decision be made? These are just a few of the areas you will need to clarify in terms of company standards.

Introductions

It's very difficult for anybody to remember a large number of people to whom they are introduced in a short time. It's especially difficult for the new employee, who is already feeling apprehensive about this new situation. Your employee can be effectively introduced to the other employees of the company through a three-step process:

1) Take the employee around the company to introduce him or her to the members of the department and to other people with whom the employee will work directly.

2) Introduce or announce the addition of the new employee through such means as a company-wide meeting or the company newsletter.

3) Encourage other employees to introduce themselves when they have the opportunity.

Problems to avoid during orientation

Just as in the hiring process itself, there are several problems you can run into during employee orientation. Following are six specific areas that can cause difficulties:

1) *Providing too much information at one time:* A common problem encountered by many employees during orientation sessions is information overload. There is no way they can be expected to retain all of it. In fact, sometimes new employees will come away from the orientation session wondering if they will be able to remember anything they were told. This creates anxiety and can make continued training extremely difficult. What can you do? Provide only the essentials and don't go into too much detail. Provide the same information verbally first and then in written form as well (e.g., in an employee handbook). Watch for nonverbal cues that indicate the new employee is feeling lost, and backtrack if necessary. You certainly can't expect your new employee to recite to you, verbatim, everything you covered during orientation. You can, however, take steps to ensure that retention is as high as possible.

2) *Failure to use demonstration and involvement:* Teachers know that their students will learn and retain more if they are actively involved in the learning experience. Take a minute to think about it. Would it be easier to learn how to bake a cake by simply reading the recipe or by reading the recipe and actually performing the steps? In orientation, you will be much further ahead with the new employee if you involve him or her as much as possible in the areas you cover. For instance, if you are trying to explain how the company's product is manufactured, wouldn't it be more effective to actually take the employee through the plant, pointing out the various steps in the production process as they are being performed? Similarly, it will be much easier for the employee to understand what his or

her department does by actually observing co-workers as they carry out their daily tasks.

3) *Lack of patience:* Most supervisors have more work to do than they can accomplish in an eight-hour day. It's not uncommon for an orientation session to be viewed as an imposition and for a supervisor to try to rush the employee through it as quickly as possible. This is a short-sighted maneuver. Time spent now will pay off, with dividends, in the future. If you fail to adequately cover something during employee orientation, you can be sure that it will come back to haunt you, and you will have to spend more time clarifying and re-explaining than you would have spent if you had done it thoroughly in the first place.

4) *Lack of preparation:* Know what you want to accomplish and how you're going to accomplish it. Have the materials you need gathered together and organized in the sequence in which they will be presented. If you appear disorganized or confused, you will not only lose some of your credibility; you will also lose the attention of your new employee.

5) *Not allowing for feedback:* Don't just assume that the new employee is understanding and assimilating every fact you present. Ask. Build in opportunities for feedback on everything you intend to cover. Stop occasionally and ask, "Do you understand our procedure on _____?" Or, better yet, ask the new employee to explain, in his or her own words, the specific procedure or company policy you just covered. Allow for and encourage questions. You want to do it right the first time so you don't have to redo it later.

6) *Failure to reduce tension:* If you fail to put your new employee at ease, all is for naught. After you've hired a good employee, orientation truly is the number-one ingredient in assuring positive performance. Make sure you use your new resource as fully as possible. Make every step in the orientation process count!

Goals, roles, and reporting lines

Marla felt her first three months working for Acme Construction were a nightmare. The training had been minimal, introductions had been non-existent; the simple process of finding the break room (and the appropriate time to use it) had seemed like an almost insurmountable hurdle. After three months, while she finally felt somewhat acclimated, she resented the wasted time and effort she had spent in a trial and error process that she felt was heavy on error.

Mark, on the other hand, found that after only a few weeks on the job with XYZ Insurance, he had a good grip on what was expected of him and why. He liked his job, understood how the functions for which he was responsible supported the functions of his coworkers' jobs, and how, collectively, they fed the success of the organization. If asked, Mark wouldn't think there was anything unique about his situation. He had received exactly the kind of direction he expected from a new supervisor. Marla could tell him how special his situation was, however. Unfortunately, her experience represents the rule rather than the exception in new-employee orientation.

When a new employee reports to work, he or she comes with many expectations. The supervisor is the person responsible for meeting those expectations, yet many times the supervisor fails to indoctrinate the employee quickly and effectively into the organization.

Orienting new employees presents a double challenge: the new employee can't ask pertinent questions because he or she isn't familiar enough to know what he or she doesn't know — and you can't answer those unasked questions. The keys to success in orienting new employees to their jobs are anticipation and simplification.

There is a tendency to take a lot for granted without even realizing that you're doing it. It is critical that you attempt to view the situation from the new hire's perspective, and realize that things that seem a matter of common sense to you aren't so obvious to the new employee.

There are three critical areas on which the supervisor must focus in the early stages: goals, roles, and reporting lines. Let's look at each of these areas in more detail.

Goals

You hire an employee because you're too busy to take care of everything that needs to get done. Then, when the employee starts work, you're often too busy to take the time to tell the employee what needs to get done and how to do it. You can't just plop someone down at a desk and start giving them assignments. You have to present a framework to them in which those assignments make sense as a whole, not as individual tasks. Goals are the structure of that framework.

First, explain to the employee the purpose of the job. This needs to be a comprehensive explanation. "Your job is data entry," isn't a comprehensive description of purpose. "Your job is to enter data on customer rebate amounts and energy savings, accurately and efficiently," is a better description of what needs to be done. Second, explain why the job is necessary. "The data you enter is used in reports we make to regulatory agencies, and also helps us keep track of progress on an individual and departmental basis."

Next, explain how the job is to be done. This is the technical aspect of the job and will involve familiarizing employees with the equipment and processes required to get the job done. Training needs will vary based on the skills the employee brings to the job. For instance, if you're using software with which the employee is familiar, training will focus on the format of the data you're gathering, file names, system protocol, and so on. If, however, the software you use is unfamiliar, training will have to start at a more fundamental level.

Finally, explain how success will be measured. "These are the ways in which I will measure your performance; this is how I'll know you're doing a good job; these are the signs that you are not performing up to my expectations."

Roles

The social and professional interactions between a new employee and his or her coworkers are critical to becoming effective in a new position.

Organizational charts are a good beginning when attempting to explain to employees where they fit in the hierarchical structure. The value of these charts is limited, however. The best way for employees to learn their roles and the roles of those around them is to begin working with others. You can't introduce a new employee to everyone in the company and expect that employee to remember who these people are, let alone what they do. Initiate casual introductions with the general workforce and then spend more time introducing the new employee to key people with whom they will be working. That extra time might involve staff meetings, project team assignments, or task forces. Supervisors may set up a certain period of time for the new employee to observe various functions as they are being performed. Perhaps the employee could spend a few hours each day with a different person with whom he or she will be working closely.

Follow-up time with the supervisor is important after these activities. This follow-up enables the supervisor to answer questions that may have arisen during these observational sessions. It may also allow the employee to bring up some more subjective issues, such as: "Joe seemed a bit resentful of my new duties, and I get the feeling that he did some of these things in the past. Is that true?" or "Carmen mentioned that I'd be helping her out on the XYZ project. Is that correct?"

Establishing an open, honest relationship with your new employee will allow you to address some of these more subjective and more sensitive issues.

Reporting lines

Like it or not, we are all concerned with status. New employees want to know answers to such questions as, "To whom can I delegate tasks?" "From whom do I take direction?" and "Who are the people I should treat with the utmost respect?"

A request from a manager in another department that conflicts with a more imminent assignment may receive short shrift unless you've previously indicated that this manager's requests need to be given top priority. You're not going to be able to deal with every potential question, problem, or conflict. What you can do is make it clear to your employees that you're open to their questions and make sure that you're accessible. Or, if you can't be available, designate somebody else who can serve as a mentor in your absence.

New employees are critical resources. Like the proverbial blank slate, they come to you with a clean record, minimal preconceived notions about what will be expected of them, and a sincere desire to do a good job. The supervisor's role is also critical. It's your job to turn that eager new employee into a fully functioning and productive member of your staff. You can do that by clearly and effectively covering the goals, roles, and reporting lines that shape the new position.

Maintaining ongoing contact

Training is just the beginning. The key to developing an effective and productive employee is ongoing interaction. The point to remember is that time spent now will more than pay off in the future.

In reviewing your orientation and training efforts, make sure that you have —

- provided the employee with an up-to-date job description and reviewed it with the employee, point by point;

- gathered examples of finished work products that the employee can use as guidelines or samples;

- gathered all pertinent procedural or training materials;

- ascertained the level of knowledge the employee brings to the job and taken steps to provide any necessary training;

- set tangible and measurable goals for learning and achievement, and established a process for regular follow-up to determine progress toward those goals;

- maintained an open dialogue with the employee to determine how the training process is going, backtracking when necessary; and

- allowed the employee to learn at his or her own pace.

If you are absolutely too busy to provide training yourself, designate another employee to serve as trainer and supervise these activities. Don't leave it to chance. Too many employees with good potential are not successful simply because they didn't receive the training they needed when they first began a new job.

5

COACHING AND COUNSELING

Managers play a critical role in developing and retaining employees. In fact, a survey conducted by Mastery Works, Inc., based in Annandale, Virginia, found that managers are the pivotal factor that determines whether people stay or leave an organization. Managers who get to know their employees, who respect and trust the competency of their employees, and who are aware of employees' contentment on the job, aspirations, and sense of career advancement will have a far greater chance of developing and maintaining positive working relationships with their employees.

The role of the manager is present at every stage of an employee's involvement with a company — from hiring to orientation and training, to the establishment of goals and providing feedback on those goals, to discipline and eventual disengagement (voluntary or involuntary) from the company.

At every step along the way, the effective manager is providing coaching and counseling to the employee and, through this process, is providing useful feedback about the values of the organization.

Coaching and counseling should take place, informally, on a daily basis. Sometimes it occurs by design, but it often happens by default.

In other words, even if you aren't specifically telling employees what you expect of them, or providing them with positive feedback to reward behavior that you wish to see repeated, they are constantly picking up cues from you and reacting to those cues.

"What do you expect from me?"

Did you ever ask an employee why they didn't do something and hear, "Because I didn't know that was what you wanted"? Expectations are too often unclear or even unstated. Do your employees know, specifically, what you expect of them? Do they know what they have to do to be considered high-level performers? If your employees don't know what their goals are, how can they meet them? If they don't meet their goals — or your expectations — they will not receive the recognition they so frequently crave.

Goals should not be developed in isolation and then handed down to employees as edicts. Employees should be involved in the goal-setting process. They will be more willing to work toward achievement of goals if they have been allowed to give input based on their personal experiences and aspirations. It is a standard management principle: commitment is gained through involvement. Goal development in isolation or failure to pay heed to the input of your employees are both good ways to sabotage your efforts in this area.

Establishing job standards

While job descriptions define what employees are expected to do, job standards provide detailed information on how an employee is expected to perform his or her duties. Clear standards can reduce ambiguity and provide a benchmark by which to measure an employee's contributions.

Without clear standards of performance, managers may leave themselves open to criticism from employees who feel they are being arbitrary or biased.

"What do you mean I'm only performing at a mid-range level? I thought I was doing good work!"

"I can't believe you're ranking me only a 3 out of 5. What do I need to do, anyway?"

"How come Julie got an excellent rating and I didn't? I think I do as good a job as she does!"

The problem in each of these situations? Lack of clear expectations.

The first step in developing job standards is to identify the critical aspects of the job. What elements of the position are necessary to keep the department and the company operating efficiently?

Most jobs have between three and six major areas of responsibility. When you are trying to pinpoint these responsibilities, don't focus on the routine or regular tasks that are performed, but the end result or purpose of those tasks. For instance, in a clerical position, filing would not be a major responsibility. The major responsibility would be "maintaining accurate files that are readily accessible to those who must rely on this information."

Once the areas of responsibility have been identified, three or four standards (or key results) that represent satisfactory performance levels need to be established.

A graphic design position, for example, might have the following critical elements:

➤ Meeting deadlines

➤ Spending an appropriate amount of time on each project

➤ Maximizing the effectiveness of the finished piece while staying within budget

Standards must be measurable. If they are not, they become merely subjective indications of how a job should be performed, and help neither the employee nor the manager. Effective standards use numbers, time limits, or error/rejection tolerances to establish objective measures of performance. More specifically, managers can use measures of quality, quantity, timeliness, or cost efficiency in establishing standards. Let's take a look at each.

1) *Quality:* Quality standards are usually written as tolerance for variances from the ideal. In other words, how many errors, omissions, or complaints would you tolerate over a given period of time? Depending on the task being performed, the period of time specified could be anywhere from one hour to one year. One company requires that errors or omissions in payroll changes shall not require special adjustment in more than one percent of all payroll checks issued each month. Another specifies that

"phones will be answered prior to the fourth ring. Callers on hold shall be re-contacted or connected within one minute. Message forms will include a legible name, number, and time of call."

2) *Quantity:* Suppose you manage a manufacturing department. A common standard might be, "Produce X amount of widgets in X amount of time." This is a measurable standard based on quantity of work produced.

3) *Timeliness:* Time standards can be written in terms of daily, weekly, monthly, or quarterly deadlines for task completion or amount of turnaround time permitted. For example, a company may require project reports to be submitted on the last working day of the month, including project status, budget to date, problems, causes of problems, and action plan for the next month. Another may specify that all internal correspondence must be ready for distribution not more than 16 working hours after receipt from staff.

4) *Cost efficiency:* Some positions have responsibility for meeting budgets or affecting costs. Here you would state standards in terms of a maximum dollar budget or a plus or minus variance from that stated budget.

Standards should answer such questions as, "What final results are expected?" "How well must the work be performed?" "How much work must be performed?" "When must the work be completed?" and so on.

Whenever possible, base standards on established baselines of performance, rather than estimates. Baselines can be established by asking employees to keep records, by reviewing past performance, or by checking industry standards, if available.

Once baselines have been developed, you can put into place minimum expected levels of performance. This minimum level becomes the standard and defines performance at an acceptable level. For instance, if your review scale went from 1 to 5, meeting the standard would give the employee a rating of 3.

Your next step, then, would be to define increments of excellence and increments of unacceptable performance. For each standard you develop, you will have to determine what level of performance exceeds your expectations and what level of performance fails to meet your expectations. At what level is remedial action in order? At what level will the employee be terminated?

The levels that you develop need to be clear to both you and your employees. Standards may vary from manager to manager and from organization to organization. That's all right. But standards should not vary from one employee to another within the same job.

Establishing clear goals

There are several benefits of establishing clear, quantifiable goals. Specific, measurable goals provide a sense of order and purpose for the entire company. Clear goals allow both employee and manager to develop a broader outlook on company objectives. Once goals are developed, management is better able to make decisions based on company and employee direction. Once goals begin to be achieved, the confidence of both employee and employer is increased.

Goal setting itself is a process that allows managers and employees to continually work for improvement.

Goals should be —

▶ Specific. A goal should state "increase sales by 20 percent" rather than "increase sales." It's important for goals to be measurable and specific. When organizational or departmental goals are unclear, motivation is decreased.

▶ Mutually agreed upon. You should strive to have goals mutually set by you and the employee. Once two people are working toward a common goal, you can be more confident that the goal will be accomplished.

▶ Unambiguous. When you are communicating your expectations to your employees, you need to clearly state what you want them to do. Misunderstandings increase the risk of criticism from both sides. Remember: no matter how clear you think your expectations are, others may feel otherwise. Understand that if your expectations are vague, your employees won't say, "Would you please tell me again what you want me to do? I still don't understand." You will have to encourage your employees to ask questions if they have the slightest doubt about what you expect of them.

- Difficult but achievable. The goals you set should be realistic. They should be neither too easy nor too difficult; they should be challenging yet attainable.

Following are the keys to developing effective goals:

- Identify and clarify organizational goals.

- Ensure that departmental goals and objectives are tied to organizational goals.

- Clarify the role of the employee.

- Develop job standards so employees know specifically what is expected of them.

- Require employees to participate in the goal-setting process, asking that each employee identify individual goals.

- Quantify goals. Establish specific deliverables and assign timelines for completion of each goal.

- Establish checkpoints so that goals can be monitored and adjusted as necessary, on an ongoing basis.

- Ensure that both employee and manager clearly understand what will happen when goals are met.

When establishing goals, don't overlook these key points:

1) Coordinate employees' personal goals with company goals. An employee's life is not segmented into two distinct parts: one part which runs from 5:00 p.m. to 8:00 a.m. and the other which runs from 8:01 a.m. to 4:59 p.m. An employee's life extends beyond the office — personal and professional goals are integrally intertwined. Your efforts when setting goals need to focus on personal goal achievement as well as professional achievement.

2) Coordinate company goals and employees' professional goals. Just as you cannot successfully develop employee goals without considering personal goals, you cannot develop employee goals without considering company goals. If the employee's efforts are not directed at tasks and goals that are aligned with a company's goals, nothing has been accomplished. Sometimes a manager will have goals that are divergent from the company's goals and, to meet his or her own personal agenda, will have employees working toward a different end than the company

envisions. This is always a mistake. Be sure that you know your company's goals and that you are communicating them to your employees. Be sure that their goals and the company's goals are working toward the same end.

3) Be specific about the consequences of not meeting goals. What are the consequences of failure to meet a goal? A lower rating on the employee evaluation form? A written warning? Suspension? Termination? If there is no consequence, your employees will soon feel that it really makes no difference whether they do what you ask. Be sure that you've communicated the impact of not meeting goals, and be sure that you follow through in the event that goals are not met.

Additional considerations

Here are some additional points you should consider when working with your employees to develop goals:

1) Don't keep the goals a secret. The most important element of establishing goals in the first place is to help employees understand what's expected of them so they can monitor their own performance.

2) Make sure the goals are written. Committing goals to writing makes it much more likely that they will be remembered and met.

3) Let employees participate in the measurement of their jobs. Again, don't establish an air of secrecy around the job standards you develop. Give employees ready access to your records of their performance. Allow them the opportunity to explain unusual circumstances, if necessary.

4) Give frequent progress reports or have employees generate these reports on their own. Keep employees informed of their progress on an ongoing basis. Remember, your goal is to avoid surprises at review time.

5) Allow some tolerance for error. Nobody performs at 100 percent all of the time. Don't set unrealistic expectations for your employees or make the highest category of performance ranking an impossible target.

Relationships are strengthened when people know what to expect from each other. No company can function without goals. There is nothing more frustrating to employees than not knowing how their jobs contribute to the overall working of the company. By establishing specific, quantifiable, and obtainable goals, you're taking the first step toward recognition of employee accomplishments.

Evaluating performance: "How am I doing?"

Far too many employees don't know the answer to this question — or they know the answer, but they don't know how it was derived.

After two jobs and seven years' experience in the utility industry, Joan, an engineer, enthusiastically started a new position as a product manager. "I jumped right into my job and thought I was contributing within a few weeks," she says. "At year-end, I was anxious for my review. I had been with the company for nearly seven months and had received little or no feedback." On review day, though, Joan was disappointed when her supervisor's only comment was, "All new employees receive the same rating, so here it is." "I was shocked and mad," she says. "That sure didn't do anything for my motivation."

Another employee tells of the frustration she felt with her company's unattainable rating system. The top rating was 200. "I continually asked what I had to do to get closer to 200," she says. At the beginning of the year she wrote an annual work plan tying specific goals to specific ratings — for example, pick up three new accounts for a rating of 160; four new accounts for a rating of 170; and so on. "My supervisor would not sign off on this work plan. He later told me that it was not possible to achieve those types of ratings on these projects, because they did not have enough impact on the company. In other words, no matter how hard I worked, I could never achieve a top rating — those were reserved for the 'big guys.' Very defeating."

Deb, a graphic designer in a university setting, says, "The only time they do something remotely resembling a review is when my contract is about to expire. Whoever happens to be my boss at the time makes a mad dash to throw something together that says they're happy with my performance and recommend keeping me on. They call me into the office, they hand me the review and say, 'Do you want to talk about anything?'" Even that semblance of a review doesn't happen frequently. The last time, Deb says, was about two years ago.

Is there anyone in any organization who would say, "I don't want to know what my boss expects of me," or, "I don't want to know what I need to do in order to develop"? It's not likely. Yet, far too often, managers fail to take the important step of letting employees know how they're doing.

Why? Face it. Performance evaluation can be a painful experience for both parties involved. Managers don't like to tell employees when their performance is not meeting expectations (particularly if they haven't been clear about what those expectations are!).

Cumbersome systems can also result in low compliance with performance evaluation requirements. A Conference Board spot survey of human resource directors and executives indicated that nearly 90 percent of them felt that their performance measures and management approaches needed reform. Yet Conference Board research also shows that performance evaluation can yield positive results for the organization.

For performance evaluation to be effective, managers need to do the following:

▶ *Ensure meaning:* The performance evaluation process must be clearly tied to the organization's objectives, as well as the individual's performance goals.

▶ *Be involved in the entire process:* Just as employees need to be involved in the goal-setting process, managers should be involved in the development and administration of the performance evaluation process. You should take the time to review forms, offer suggestions, and provide ongoing feedback on the system and how it contributes to employee development and satisfaction, based on your first-hand experience.

▶ *Make it ongoing:* Performance review should not be an annual event. You need to keep employees informed on an ongoing basis of how they are doing in relation to the goals that have been mutually established.

▶ *Keep it simple:* If your goal is to ensure that employees in your department participate in the performance review process, you will be more likely to achieve compliance if you avoid over-complicating the process. Consider how technology could be used to help simplify overly complex performance appraisal systems.

▶ *Take advantage of training and education on performance evaluation:* While training isn't the key to motivating managers to conduct effective performance evaluations, it is certainly an important part of the process. Seek opportunities to participate in training on how to provide feedback — positive and negative — to staff members.

➤ *Understand the big picture:* Why is performance evaluation valued by the organization? How does an individual's performance benefit the organization? How can that performance be objectively measured? What forms and tools does the organization make available to expedite this process?

Providing constructive feedback

It would seem that giving positive feedback to employees would be easy. After all, what could be challenging about telling an employee that he or she is doing a good job? Unfortunately, though, too many managers fail to take the time or make the effort — for a variety of reasons.

"My manager never notices when things are going right," says one employee who works in a busy administrative environment. "She expects things to go right."

"If I took the time to tell them every time they did something right, I'd never get anything done!" complains one manager.

"I guess he just assumes we know when we're on track," one employee muses. "After all, we know what our goals are and we get reports that tell us how we're doing. Maybe he thinks that's enough."

"You can't win," complains another manager. "If I praise one employee for a good job, I have the rest of the staff grumbling that I never recognize their work."

Most companies have formal systems in place to provide employee evaluations. Usually these evaluations take place twice a year. But while these evaluation meetings serve an important purpose, they don't fulfill an employee's need for consistent and constant feedback. You need to do more than tell them every six months that they're doing a good (or bad) job.

What can happen if you don't? Plenty. Let's look at a couple of examples.

Nancy started her job as a secretary for a small company five years ago. She was well liked, even though her performance wasn't all it could be. Because of her good personality and the family-like structure of the company, she was kept on, shifted from one job to another where her skills could be best utilized. For a time she was a receptionist because she was good on the phones. Then she served as assistant for a few people because she followed instructions well and was pleasant to work with.

During this time, Nancy was never told that her typing skills were below par. She was never told that her letter and report compositions were inadequate. She was never given the opportunity to improve. Eventually, the company grew beyond her limited means and, when it was no longer possible to find positions that were suitable for her, she was terminated. Neither Nancy nor her coworkers saw it coming, and they didn't understand when it happened. The termination was a troublesome one for Nancy, for her managers, and for her fellow employees. Long after she was gone they suffered from feelings of insecurity. "If it could happen to her, it could happen to me." "How can I tell if I'm really doing a good job?" were comments heard throughout the firm time and time again.

Had Nancy been told of her inadequacies at an early date, she could have been trained in the areas in which she was lacking. She could have grown with the company and been a valued and loyal employee. Because this didn't happen, the company was forced to let her go on acrimonious terms.

You owe it to your employees to provide feedback, not only so you can get the most productive use of them but also so they can develop their skills and grow with you.

Good employees can also be lost due to inattention.

Lainie was also hired as a secretary at a small firm and grew with the company to eventually hold a management position. She took courses at a local college to enhance her skills, joined numerous professional groups to establish her professionalism, and worked hard. Her managers valued her contributions and felt she was a model employee, but they never felt the need to tell her because she always seemed to be self-motivated.

Because Lainie never heard the positive comments she craved, she felt unappreciated. She felt that because she had been promoted from within and not hired as an expert from outside the company, eventually she would be replaced. She began to look for employment elsewhere and eventually left her job. The day she resigned was the first time she was told just how important she was to the company. Unfortunately, by then it was too late.

Nancy and Lainie represent distinct ends of a spectrum between marginal employees and stellar employees. But what about the employees that is merely acceptable? Suppose you have an employee who meets all of your expectations and does the job exactly right but isn't outstanding. You feel insincere about going out of your way to tell this employee what a great job she or he is doing. What can you do?

You can, as Ken Blanchard points out in his best-selling book *One Minute Manager,* catch your employees "doing something right." Here's an example:

> *Sam has worked at ABC Corporation for 25 years. During that time, he's had a series of managers. None have ever noticed (or recognized) him for performing any better than the other 10 members of his work group. A new manager was recently hired. After reviewing production reports and individual evaluations of worker performance, the new manager is surprised to see that Sam was a high performer during his first 13 years of employment. His performance declined, though, after his 13th year. He now works at a fair but steady pace that could most accurately be termed satisfactory.*
>
> *The new manager calls Sam into her office to talk, not about his performance, but about his interests (at home and at work). She wants to know about the things he likes about his job and about the things he dislikes. After the meeting she remarks, "Sam, your records indicate that you have consistently been one of ABC's best employees. I hope you will keep up the good work."*
>
> *She continues these individual meetings and always makes a special effort to comment on any increase in Sam's output. In a relatively short period of time, Sam's level of performance is exceeding the point it had been at 12 years earlier!*

Sam's manager took the time to catch Sam "doing something right." The end result? Sam was recognized.

Here's another example:

> *Suzanne was excellent in her position as sales clerk in a large department store. In fact, she was so good that she*

was quickly promoted to the position of women's wear sales manager. In this position she was responsible for a large staff of other sales clerks.

As sales manager, however, Suzanne quickly lost the drive she had had as a clerk. She no longer felt the personal reward that accompanied a large sale. She was also growing envious of others in her department who seemed to get all the credit while she merely monitored results.

One day Suzanne had the opportunity to speak to the store manager about this problem. The store manager listened closely and assured Suzanne that her problem wasn't unique. Several other department sales managers felt very much the same way.

A few weeks later, the store manager called all the managers together. He told them about a new program the store was implementing: sales teams. Each department manager would be responsible for a team of salespeople. Managers were responsible for encouraging and motivating members of their team to increase sales. After a three-month trial period, a reward system would be established. Each month a specific department would be recognized for outstanding sales achievement.

The new system was, in effect, no different from the old system. The store manager had been smart enough to realize that it wasn't enough for department sales managers to watch their staff succeed. Managers needed to feel that they played an important part in this achievement.

Six months later the store's sales had increased dramatically. Department sales managers felt better about the work they were doing and the role they played in improving sales. Department members felt part of a team with a clear goal in mind. The monthly reward dinners were also well accepted. In short, the managers and their staff were recognized.

If you want to get the same kind of action and see the same results from the people you manage, you should recognize them frequently, sincerely, and consistently.

If you think about it, we're all trying to be recognized, whether we're putting on a new suit or presenting a major proposal. When you're dealing with employees, recognition is extremely important. In fact, almost every aspect of employee reward — monetary or non-monetary — is a function of recognition.

Everyone likes recognition. However, not every employee will want to be recognized in the same way. The effect of recognition, therefore, will depend on —

- ➤ the achievement for which the employee is recognized,
- ➤ how the employee is recognized, and
- ➤ how often the employee is recognized.

As a manager, it's up to you to examine these variables and determine how they apply to each of your employees. Remember, the achievement for which you recognize an employee and how you recognize that employee are as important as providing recognition in the first place.

Giving credit and praise for accomplishments

What happens when employees in your department meet or exceed the goals you have set?

Your answer should be: "I praise them."

There is no such thing as a self-motivator. Each of us is motivated by something and, for many of us, that something is praise.

Fail to praise your employees and they will fail to perform. They will fail to perform time after time after time, until you either replace them or they seek employment elsewhere. The end result, of course, is that you have lost a potentially good employee.

We get what we reward. When we praise employees we are providing positive reinforcement for their actions. Subtly or not so subtly, this reinforcement ensures that the action will be repeated. When we ignore a positive action or behavior by failing to provide positive reinforcement, what message do we send?

Managers should ask themselves, "What is my action (or inaction) saying to subordinates about what is of secondary or no importance to me?" Managers need to make sure that each person in the organization knows they have a unique contribution to make.

When do you offer praise? The answer to this question relates directly to establishing employee goals. You offer praise when an employee has met or exceeded one of the requirements you have established together. And, when this circumstance arises, you should offer praise immediately.

The question of immediacy is one that relates directly to performance review. Some managers feel they are doing a good job of documenting the positive behaviors and actions of employees by jotting a note in the employee file so that the action can be noted when review time comes. How much impact do you think praise will have when it occurs weeks, or months, after the behavior? Very little. However, when you consistently note and comment on achievements and accomplishments as soon as they happen, the effect on morale and productivity is substantial.

Another key to effective motivation is providing specific feedback. If your administrative assistant stays late to finish an important report and you mumble "thanks" as you rush out the door, is your assistant to assume that the report is well formatted, the report was prepared in a timely manner, or the report contained few typographical errors?

In fact, your assistant will have no idea what you mean unless you say what you mean.

"Thank you for staying late to finish this report. I appreciated your dedication and dependability." These words would convey to your assistant specifically what you mean by "good job."

Sincerity is also crucial. The people who work for you will be able to tell immediately whether your comments are sincere or meaningless. Giving praise simply because you know you should is not enough. You need to be giving praise because you honestly believe that a good job was done.

Unfortunately, not all employees are good (or even marginal) performers. Some employees have performance problems that must be addressed. How can you address those problems in a positive way?

The importance of constructive feedback

Discipline is not necessarily a negative event. In fact, criticism can be either positive or negative. Positive criticism — or constructive feedback — focuses on identifying causes of unsatisfactory behavior and changing the behavior to help the employee improve. The supervisor asks the question, "How can we make this situation better?"

Negative criticism, conversely, is a reaction to an unsatisfactory behavior that involves lashing out and placing blame. The supervisor takes the approach of teaching the employee a lesson. The thought process is: punish first, then ask why.

Negative criticism results in defensive and emotional reactions by the subordinate. The employee feels attacked and, in the short term, his or her behavior will include withdrawal and avoidance. In the long term, the undesired behavior will usually recur. You've treated the symptom but not the problem. In short, negative criticism is a short-term solution that —

➤ creates ill will,

➤ slows motivation and productivity,

➤ affects the use of positive discipline in the future, and

➤ doesn't yield the changes you want.

Constructive feedback, however, is an employee development tool. The worst thing a manager can do to an employee is to pretend that a problem doesn't exist. Unfortunately, many managers do just that. In their efforts to avoid unpleasant confrontations, they begin to ignore these workers. Unattended problems will not go away. Instead, they tend to accumulate and multiply. The performance of an employee who is getting no recognition or feedback at all is unlikely to improve.

But, even though many managers recognize this, offering constructive feedback is challenging. As difficult as it can be to give positive acknowledgement to employees, constructive feedback can be several times more difficult. However, it is crucial that you know how to effectively provide this feedback to your employees so they can learn and grow in their positions.

Why do managers avoid criticizing employees? There can be a number of reasons. They may be afraid of offending the employee and harming the relationship. They may be worried about starting a full-blown argument. They may not want to seem petty or unreasonable. In today's litigious environment, they may even be concerned that they might create a risk of legal action. Much of our hesitance about criticism stems from our childhoods. For many of us, the following beliefs are engrained:

➤ "He or she will no longer like me."

➤ "If you can't say something nice, say nothing."

➤ "People cannot take criticism."

Let's examine these excuses.

1) "He or she will no longer like me." Being a supervisor or manager is not a popularity contest. Of course, you would rather have employees like you than dislike you. What you really need as a supervisor, though, is respect — and motivated employees. You get neither if you fail to provide timely and valid criticism.

2) "If you can't say something nice, say nothing." It's possible that your parents told you this when you were quite young and your interpersonal contacts were limited to the playground. As a supervisor, however, this rule is not sensible. Following it could result in never speaking to some employees!

3) "People cannot take criticism." People need criticism, especially your employees. Without criticism, you cannot expect your employees to improve their behavior, their performance, or their motivation. What this statement really means is, "People cannot take unfounded criticism."

Unresolved disciplinary issues can have a negative impact on the organization in many ways. There may be direct dollar costs. Incompetence may cause inefficiencies, may result in damage to company equipment, may contribute to the loss of customers or clients, or may result in costly errors. There may be productivity costs. Work bottlenecks may be created since most jobs interrelate with others. You, as supervisor, may find yourself having to spend more of your time on training, counseling, and disciplining this one employee while the rest of your job is put on hold.

There will almost certainly be morale problems, especially if you fail to take action. Other employees will quickly become irritated if someone in their workgroup is not pulling his or her weight and is, in effect, getting away with it.

You will also more than likely have problems with upper management. In fact, if you allow incompetence to go unchecked, your own work record will be tarnished.

Sometimes you will be in the position of giving feedback to someone else. Recognize how difficult hearing this information may be. The following tips may be helpful in getting your point across without damaging your relationship:

► Ask if the individual is willing to hear your feedback. As managers, we are expected to provide feedback, but often we want to give feedback to people for whom we are not formally responsible.

Before sharing your thoughts, ask if the individual is open to your feedback. If he or she is not, keep your comments to yourself.

➤ Be specific. When providing feedback, focus on the task. Don't get personal. Be as specific as you can, giving examples whenever possible and clearly explaining how your feedback can help improve a process, service, or other work-related activity.

➤ Allow time for response. Expect silence as the immediate response to your feedback. It can take a while for the information to sink in. Clarify if necessary.

➤ Say "thank you." Just as when receiving feedback, it's important to indicate to the individual you've provided feedback to that you appreciate the opportunity to share your viewpoint.

➤ Follow up. Your job isn't over after you've shared your feedback. To ensure a change in behavior, you need to check in regularly with the employee.

Giving and receiving feedback can be threatening, but it is a critical aspect of any work relationship. With practice, time, and a firm commitment to viewing feedback as an objective means of improving work performance — and not a personal attack — you can learn to gather information that will help you learn and grow in your position.

Handling problem employees

Habits that require disciplinary action don't develop overnight. In most cases, the supervisor should have been able to spot early warning signs well in advance of the need for desperate action. Spotting a problem at an early stage allows the opportunity for positive counseling and intervention before a major crisis develops. Watch for signs that an employee may have, or may be developing, a performance problem. For example, an employee might —

➤ show a decline in performance,

➤ be apathetic or withdrawn,

➤ complain about trivial aspects of the job,

➤ create difficulties in working relationships with managers,

➤ refuse or be reluctant to discuss the problem,

➤ have continuing interpersonal problems with others in the organization,

- resent criticism, or

- exhibit behavior that negatively affects others in the work group.

After these initial warning signals, the problem typically becomes more serious. At this stage you will be faced with some very common causes for discipline: absence without leave, disobedience, insubordination, or non-performance of job duties. When an employee problem has reached this stage, it's a sign that you've waited too long to take action.

Once a problem has been identified, it's time for you to take action. But before you do, there are several questions that you will need to ask yourself:

- Did the employee know and understand the rule that was broken or the procedure that was not followed?

- Was the employee warned of possible disciplinary consequences?

- Is the rule or procedure that was violated necessary for the orderly, efficient, and safe operation of the business?

- Was a fair and objective investigation conducted to determine whether the employee actually violated the rule?

- Has the company applied rules, procedures, and penalties fairly and consistently to all employees?

You must determine all the facts before having a discussion with the errant employee. If you don't, you may find that your decision to discipline was incorrect and you have alienated the employee.

Let's assume that you have a problem employee who, it has been reported, is consistently coming in late and has been intimidating other employees into covering up for this tardiness. Before you confront the employee, you may need to consult:

- the person(s) making the report,

- other employees,

- your immediate supervisor, and

- the human resources department.

You will want to gather all of the facts and be as specific as possible in terms of:

- What happened?

- When did it happen?
- How often did it happen?
- Who knew it happened?

You will want to review this employee's past history to determine length of service, specifics of past performance, and the possibility of other disciplinary actions.

You should compare this situation with other similar situations that have occurred at your company. What have other supervisors done with employees who have exhibited the same or a similar problem? What have you done in similar situations?

You will want to know the answers to these questions:

- Who was involved in the incident?
- What led up to the incident?
- What feelings were expressed by those involved?

After you have gathered all the facts, you will want to analyze the situation to determine the following:

- How the involved parties (and you) may have contributed to the problem
- How the involved parties (and you) can contribute to a solution
- Whether there are differing perceptions and misunderstandings contributing to the problem
- To what extent outside forces influenced the problem
- The probability that a meaningful improvement can be obtained in the near future

Exercising positive discipline

Douglas McGregor formulated what he called the "hot stove rule" as the basis for implementing positive discipline. His theory is that effective discipline is analogous to touching a hot stove. When you touch a stove, the consequences are immediate, impersonal, predictable, and consistent. When your hand is burned you know immediately that you have done something wrong. The fact that you were burned is a function of the stove — it is not a function of who you are or of any aspect of your personality. Every time you touch the stove you will be burned.

The same thing would happen to anyone who touched the stove regardless of their age, sex, or attitudes.

Effective discipline incorporates the same principles: immediacy, predictability, impersonality, and consistency.

1) *Immediacy:* When discipline is necessary, you should approach the employee as soon as possible after the violation has been noticed or reported. At this point, the incident will be fresh in both your mind and the employee's mind. If you wait too long, the impact of your confrontation will be lessened. You should, however, time your confrontation so that you approach the employee at the optimum time. For instance, you don't want to corner the employee the minute he or she comes to work on Monday morning or just as he or she is leaving on a Friday afternoon. When you do approach the employee, you should immediately state your concern in as few words as possible, and let the employee know that a rule or order has been violated.

2) *Predictability:* The employee should be well aware that the behavior he or she exhibited was in violation of some company rule or previous order. It should be very clear that anyone exhibiting that behavior would be disciplined. In dealing with a subsequent infraction, then, the employee will be well aware that he or she has violated a rule or previous order and will not be surprised by the action you take.

3) *Impersonality:* Employees sometimes feel as though their supervisors are out to get them. It's important that your employees know that when they are disciplined, it is because of what they did and not who they are. You should be just as willing to approach one of your star performers with a performance issue as you are one of your problem employees. When practicing positive discipline, it is important that you do not treat your employee as an adversary and that you address the issue civilly without lecturing or losing your temper. Let the employee tell his or her side of the story. Ask questions only to obtain details. Listen with an open mind and give the employee the benefit of the doubt.

4) *Consistency:* It is extremely important that you and the company you work for are consistent in your discipline of employees. To determine the appropriate course of action to take, you should find out how other employees were treated in similar

circumstances. Talk to other supervisors, the personnel or human resources manager, or others knowledgeable about company policy and precedent. Both because you want employees to be treated fairly and because you want to avoid legal liability, you should make every possible effort to ensure that your disciplinary actions are consistent.

When you meet with an employee who needs to be disciplined, there are several things you must keep in mind and several steps you should have already taken. As we've seen previously, you should have gathered as many facts as possible about the situation. Also, you should have reviewed the employee's personnel file to determine if this behavior has occurred in the past. In addition, you should make sure that the employee is well aware of the reason for this meeting.

When you meet, you should:

➤ Have notes and make use of them.

➤ Explain the facts you have gathered as fully as possible.

➤ Ask the employee to give his or her perspective. Allow the opportunity for some emotional venting.

➤ Discuss the situation in depth with the employee and explore various ways the situation might have been handled differently.

➤ Make a determination, in your own mind, as to whether discipline is justified.

➤ Explain what you intend to do and why — refer to company policy and precedent. Try to obtain the employee's agreement that he or she has done something wrong and that discipline is necessary.

➤ Be very specific about what the consequence will be for continued infractions.

➤ Provide a system for follow-up. Be specific about how future behavior will be monitored, what results you expect, and how you expect the employee (with your help) to obtain them.

Here are some additional guidelines for ensuring positive discipline:

➤ Give fair warning. Let the employee know that his or her behavior is inappropriate.

➤ Listen to the employee's side until you fully understand the motivation for the behavior.

- Deal with the objective issues and not your own subjective emotions and feelings. Say, "When you're late, you create additional work for others in the department"; not: "You're totally irresponsible and you make me look like a poor manager when you come in late every day."

- Discipline privately. Make every possible effort to avoid embarrassing the employee in front of others.

- Be sure to find out how the employee feels about the action you are taking. Does he or she feel that you are being fair?

- Be sure to obtain the employee's commitment to improve.

- Document the incident in writing and include it in the employee's personnel file.

Coaching and counseling are critical managerial functions. Without feedback and the occasional course correction, employees cannot perform effectively — and they will not be motivated. While managers may wish to avoid offering criticism of any kind, the reality is that employees appreciate the effort. If you believe that your employees want to do a good job — and why would an employee not want to do a good job? — then, obviously, your feedback is crucial. You need to make an effort to tell employees what they're doing right and you need to overcome any reluctance to provide course correction when warranted.

Exit Interviews

Whether an employee is leaving your company on voluntary or involuntary terms, exit interviews can be a valuable way to get information about your organization — good and bad — at a critical point in an employee's tenure. To be effective, though, exit interviews must be carefully planned, consistently administered, and thoroughly analyzed.

Exit interviews should be a standard operating practice

Make all employees aware that exit interviews are part of the separation process and an important source of information for the company. Doing so will ensure that employees won't be taken by surprise when asked to participate in an interview and will understand that the purpose is not negative or subversive, but to improve the company's operations and management style.

Use an objective third party to conduct the interview

Exit interviews can be very sensitive. Employees may be hesitant to share candid information for fear that they may hamper their chances for a good future reference or for future employment with the company. The human resource department can provide the necessary objectivity to lessen these fears. If this isn't possible, ask another manager in the organization to conduct the interview.

Conduct an in-person interview

While some companies use a written exit interview form and ask the departing employee to complete and return it at their convenience, a face-to-face interview can be more effective and will yield immediate information. (Some employees may never return a written form.)

Look for trends, not incidents

Avoid the tendency to overreact to feedback. An isolated negative comment about a company policy or management practice should not lead to an immediate change. Instead, watch for trends over the long term. If turnover is higher in a certain department and exit interviews point consistently to management issues, that's a trend that deserves attention.

Here are some questions that can help yield the actionable information you're looking for:

> ► Why are you leaving? What about the company/position you're going to interests you?

> ► Are there any practices or working conditions here that led or contributed to your decision to seek work elsewhere?

> ► Did you feel that your position here had a significant impact on our organization? Why or why not?

> ► What did you like and/or not like about your relationship with your manager?

> ► What did you like and/or not like about your relationship with your coworkers?

> ► Are there any particular policies or activities in place here that you feel are important to maintaining a positive work environment? Why?

- ▸ Do you feel there are any particular policies or activities that we do not currently practice, but which could contribute to a more positive work environment?

- ▸ What can we do to ensure that your replacement will have a positive experience here?

Coaching and counseling are ongoing responsibilities of small-business owners and managers. These activities should occur not once a year, but on a daily basis. Managing employees is all about relationships. Your relationships with employees will be strengthened by providing frequent, honest, and constructive feedback.

6

COMMUNICATION

The development and establishment of clear, realistic, and measurable goals is an important element in maintaining a motivated workforce. Establishing goals isn't enough, however. Those goals must be clearly communicated and that communication must become a continuous process.

One of the basic tenets of McGregor's Theory Y, discussed in chapter 1, is: "People are important." And, what's one of the best ways to let people know they're important? Tell them.

Communication, whether for praise, criticism, or information, is an important motivational factor. It's amazing, then, that while we're in the midst of an information explosion, our organizational communications are so often faulty or ineffective.

In the Work Canada Survey, Watson Wyatt Canada surveyed 2004 working Canadians from all job levels and a wide variety of industries to measure how well the organizations were doing at aligning employees with their strategies and goals. Survey results indicated the following:

> ► Only 34 percent of employees said their organizations did a good job of seeking their opinions.

> ► Only 33 percent felt that their management made good decisions.

► Only 39 percent said their organizations fostered continuous employee growth.

Even at the smallest organization and even with the highest level of commitment from top management, the task of communicating effectively to employees can be complex. The environment in which you do business changes and, as those changes occur, communication needs shift. New threats appear. New challenges are presented. New issues arise. A change in upper management — particularly at the very top of an organization — can cause a shift in organizational culture. A merger, buy-out, reorganization, or downsizing can challenge even the most skillful communicators. Just one manager who fails to live by the corporate communication model can have a dramatic negative effect on trust — and can threaten even the most skillfully planned and carefully executed communication efforts.

Fortunately, even though the challenges are great, there are certain common characteristics and a measure of consistency that can be found in organizations that are known for effectively communicating with their employees.

Communication: An organizational priority

Kerry Liberman is founder of People Perspectives, a company specializing in employee satisfaction surveys and consulting. "Interestingly," Liberman says, "I think managers often fall into the trap of believing that communication and feedback are not critical to employees' job satisfaction." Employees, she says are more apt to leave an organization if managers do not communicate with them very often or do not make themselves accessible. "All of us like to have support and feedback at some level from our managers. If we don't get it, it can often provide a compelling reason to look for another job."

It starts at the top

Donald Sheppard, CEO of Sheppard Associates, the world's largest independent consulting agency specializing in internal communication strategy, implementation, training, measurement, and management, says that employee communication starts with clarification of the organization's mission. Therefore, you must start at the top. "The people who own the messages own the vision," he says. "The senior leaders articulate that — not corporate communication or HR."

If you are responsible for managing employees, you need to be intimately aware of your organization's key messages. Are you? Or are the expectations that you have for your employees based on your own personal objectives and beliefs? The role of the manager in any organization is to take the message that has been framed by upper management and ensure that it is communicated frequently, consistently, and effectively throughout the organization.

The organization itself often participates in or leads these efforts through the use of such tools as the employee newsletter, the company intranet, or employee meetings. As a manager, you can take a cue from these organizational tools, sharing key messages with employees.

Preparing employees to hear the messages

While top management is clearly the critical first step in any effective employee communication initiative, managers play a pivotal support role. It's not enough to have top management articulate messages to be sent to employees if the employees aren't prepared to receive the messages.

Maslow's hierarchy of needs is a model that is as applicable to employee communication as it is to employee motivation. Employees won't be ready to move to higher levels of understanding until their basic-level needs — for safety, security, and belonging — are met.

A new employee, for example, will not be ready to hear about the organization's goals and how he or she helps to further those goals, until that new employee fully understands some of the basics of the job — how much he or she will be paid, the benefits he or she will receive, even such simple things as where the lunchroom is located and when break times are.

An employee's security needs may be impacted by organizational changes. For example, during a restructuring or reorganization, employees will become highly concerned about the impact of the change on their jobs and livelihoods (security), and will be less able to focus on higher-level messages that the company may be trying to communicate. Until the employee understands how he or she will be affected, he or she is unlikely to care about how the reorganization will positively impact the organization, and will be less receptive to those messages.

Employees' affiliation needs also come into play. Employees have a need to feel that they are an important part of the overall organization.

Only once these basic-level needs — the need for security and belonging — are met will employees be ready to hear broader organizational messages.

Organizations can measure and monitor employee needs through focus groups and surveys and identify areas where training or intervention may be appropriate. If employees are focused on concerns about being downsized, they are unlikely to be able to focus on corporate messages.

Once these basic-level needs have been met, employees need to understand how they fit in. The need for contribution becomes more prevalent and employees want a sense of how they are having an impact on the company.

Finally, employees are ready to move to the top levels of the hierarchy and become concerned about the organization.

The manager's challenge is to guide the employee toward meeting the needs of the organization by focusing on the employee's individual concerns.

Manager as role model

Managers are role models. Employees watch you. They pay close attention to both what you say and what you do. And, when those two behaviors don't match up, guess which one they trust? They trust what you do. For communication efforts to be effective, you must demonstrate through your words, deeds, policies, practices, and procedures that you are, indeed, practicing what you preach.

That means sharing the bad with the good — no sugar coating. If you don't, the rumor mill will beat you every time — and, much of the time, the rumor mill is true. One of the best ways to beat the rumor mill is through direct communication. Face-to-face communication builds trust and credibility while ensuring that employees are receiving consistent messages.

This can be a challenge for managers who are responsible for large numbers of employees or for employees working multiple shifts. The best solution to this problem is to combine face-to-face communication with other techniques. Alternative communication techniques might include —

> ► an open forum on your company intranet site,

- ► regularly scheduled group meetings at times that are convenient for all shifts and that are offered at all locations where you have employees,

- ► the appointment of assistants whose responsibility is to convey messages to their work teams, and

- ► frequent memos or written updates sent out to staff.

The point is to get the word out through a combination of channels, never forgetting that face-to-face communication will always be the most effective.

Front-line managers are critical to successful communication. The closer you are to the employees, the more impact your messages have. But you're not the only source of information. Take advantage of every communication tool your company has to offer. Use multiple tools, multiple channels, multiple ways — the more opportunities you can provide for employees to receive key messages, the more likely you are to connect with them.

Communicating in an environment of change

The idea that change is a constant is becoming a cliché. No matter what industry you work in, by now you've accepted the fact that the only certainty is that nothing will stay the same for very long. That's not necessarily a bad thing. If our environment didn't change, we would still be riding horses, washing our clothes in fast-moving streams, and growing our own food.

There is no doubt, however, that the pace of change has rapidly accelerated over the last few decades. And there should be no question that the pace of change will not slow in the new millenium. In fact, today's leaders must be able to effectively lead their organizations through change — and be able to maintain that change over time (at least until the next opportunity for change comes along).

Consider two types of change: one personal and one organizational. First, think about a very commonly experienced personal change process: going on a diet. Second, think about an equally common professional experience: learning to use a new software program. What does it require for an individual to achieve success with these changes?

1) *A clear vision:* When you go on a diet you probably have a good idea of what the end result of that diet will be. You can picture yourself being a different size, perhaps different proportions — you know specifically where you're headed. What about when you're learning a new software program? Your vision might be of yourself mastering the program and using it to do some task that will help you be more efficient, productive, and effective. For managers, that vision might be the automation of a complicated process or the restructuring of a work unit.

2) *A reason to believe:* Diets tend to become fads as one individual's positive experience leads to another's adoption of the techniques used to achieve the positive change. You are unlikely to go on a diet without some evidence that it works. The reason to believe is an important part of making the decision to embark on any change process. The same is true of learning a new software program. Without evidence that you will be more efficient at your job once the program is mastered, there is little reason to change your work habits.

   As a leader, your challenge is providing employees with a reason to believe in the end result when, in many cases, you may be exploring new, uncharted, territory.

3) *A plan:* Your vision may be so forward-looking that there is not a great deal of tangible evidence to provide to employees to convince them that they should follow you. The "protein diet" has become popular in recent years. But to achieve success with this diet requires more than general knowledge that you should increase your intake of protein and decrease your intake of carbohydrates. To be successful, you need some sort of plan — in this case a diet plan — to guide you along the path to success. Knowing that you need to learn a new software program doesn't do much to help you make this professional change. You need a good idea of how this transition will occur. As a leader, it's not enough to say, "This is my vision; this is where we're headed." Your staff wants to know, "How do we get from here to there?" And, very often, they want to know specifically. You may not know the answers to these questions. But the more guidance you can provide and the more clearly you are able to outline your plan, the more committed your staff will be.

4) *Observable results:* How long would you maintain a change in your eating habits without some evidence that your efforts were paying off? Probably not very long. A diet, like any change, requires certain sacrifices and results in certain discomforts. Change isn't easy. It takes effort. Individuals are not likely to put forth effort over an extended period of time without some evidence that their personal sacrifice is having a positive impact. Similarly, when learning a new software program, if you discover that it is more difficult to use than the old program, and took more time to accomplish the same goals, how long (given a choice) would you maintain that change? How long after a downsizing, reorganization, restructuring, or introduction of a new product will employees remain committed without evidence of success?

5) *Success:* What determines whether you will stay on your diet? Early success — seeing those first pounds slip off and noticing the difference in the way your clothes fit and the way you look. Positive reinforcement — receiving compliments and encouragement from friends. A personal sense of accomplishment — that good feeling that comes from knowing you've been successful at a goal you've established for yourself. The same elements apply to any type of change.

Creating an environment for change

Daryl Conner, author of *Managing at the Speed of Change* and *Leading at the Edge of Chaos: How to Create the Nimble Organization,* agrees. "Change now breeds itself," he says, so the challenge is, "how do we deal with perpetual unrest?"

It's not always an easy task, but it's not an impossible one. It becomes more challenging as organizations grow and become more complex, but the principles of guiding change remain the same, whether dealing with personal change, change for a small department, or change for a large organization.

The concept of the nimble organization is key to Conner's work. In fact, the first line of *Leading at the Edge of Chaos* reads, "The focal point for this book is leadership's role in building resilient, nimble organizations." Organizations that are not nimble, Conner says, are constrained. To build nimble organizations, according to Conner, leaders "must bring to the human side of change the same levels of rigor and discipline that are applied to the organization's financial assets."

Leadership sets the stage and determines the culture for the nimble organization. "Responsibility begins at the board/governance level, with the formal recognition of nimbleness as a strategic imperative," says Conner. "It continues at the senior leadership level, with executives taking steps to prepare themselves and their organization for ongoing change."

The paradox for leaders is that, while they need to have a clearly articulated vision, they also need to be prepared to react quickly to a constantly changing business and social environment. And they have to find ways to engage their employees in these change initiatives. Communicating a culture of change can help. What are the keys to promoting such a culture?

1) *Having a vision:* "If you don't know where you're going, any map will take you there," goes a popular aphorism, and the logic is sound. A vision helps you guide the organization and provides your staff members with a clear idea of where you — and they — are headed.

2) *Hiring and retaining those individuals who are change resilient:* These employees are not always easy to find, especially in a tight economy. But they are out there. Conner says, "Hire people that are capable of performing the duties of the job, hire people that resonate with the values you have in your culture, and hire people whose instincts and life experiences have guided them toward being a resilient person."

3) *Energizing the staff:* Try to let everybody be a cheerleader for something. Allow employees to play a part in the facilitation of change by letting them participate in the change process — all the way from management down to front-line staff. We support what we create. Let your employees help to create change so that they will ultimately support that change.

4) *Constantly communicating the vision and reinforcing the culture:* Jack Welch, CEO of GE, speaks of the "relentless drum beat" — the need to continually speak of your vision and to ensure that it is reinforced in everything you say, do, and believe. Talk about it. Talk about it. Talk about it.

Once employees understand your organization's vision and have the capacity and the enthusiasm to navigate whatever change you're embarking on, it's time to get out of the way and let them do their jobs. And when they do, it's important to recognize and reward their efforts. A change process is difficult to sustain if those involved aren't provided with cues along the way that they are headed in the right direction. Those cues include feedback and, when appropriate, celebration.

These tactics seem very straightforward. Why is it, then, that so many organizations fail in their change efforts?

Conner uses an analogy of a sponge. A sponge will only hold so much liquid before the liquid starts to roll off. Like sponges, Conner says, "every organization has a certain capacity to absorb change." When the organization tries to take on too much change at one time, "you start to have future-shock symptoms," he says. People can't absorb any more change without exhibiting dysfunctional behaviors.

"Most organizations," Conner points out, "pour too much change into the system. They tend to implement all of their good ideas. What we suggest is you probably have more good ideas that you can afford. Focus on business imperatives. You actually have to learn how to say no to things that intellectually make sense."

Organizations have two imperatives, according to Conner: to be protective of whatever absorption capacity they have, and/or to increase sponge capacity. You increase the capacity of the sponge in three ways:

1) By hiring resilient people

2) By teaching the dynamics of change

3) By providing employees with structured tools and a disciplined approach to whatever the change entails

You protect the sponge by developing the capacity to say "no" to the things you wish you could say "yes" to. The changes that take place in most organizations, he says, are good ideas. Yet, very often, reengineering efforts, SAP implementations, mergers, and other interventions have terrible track records. "When you look back," he says, "it's not because it was the wrong technology or the wrong merger partner — it was because we had 15,000 other changes going on."

What you should tell employees

An organization needs to communicate to promote understanding, productivity, and a team identity. As a manager or supervisor, you need to communicate —

- ► the rules and policies of the organization,
- ► information on current organizational activities,
- ► reviews of past results, mistakes in judgment, and goal accomplishment, and
- ► progress, organizational plans, and corporate objectives.

Why should you tell your employees these things? Because involvement is an important determinant of motivation and, ultimately, productivity. If your people don't know where the company is going, where it's been, or why you're asking them to do certain things, they can't be productive. They have no idea of how what they do fits into the larger picture. Your job is to give them an idea of how they fit in. Then you need to keep giving them that information so they will continue to produce.

A manager's job is 90 percent communication. It's not hard to understand, then, why poor communication is a major business problem today. Poor communication is at the root of almost every business problem, from low productivity to employee theft. Communication is the giving and receiving of information needed for intelligent actions or decisions. It is also an act of creating understanding between individuals.

There can be several reasons for poor communication. It may be the result of ego or self-interest. You may feel that certain things are not important enough to communicate. Or perhaps listening is the problem; because we all prefer to talk rather than listen, efforts to communicate may not get heard or we may incorrectly interpret the things we hear. Perhaps the most deep-rooted barrier to communication, however, is simply the failure to see the need for it.

Lack of proper communication has far-reaching effects for any business. These effects may include the following:

- ► Good ideas that are not implemented because they were not heard
- ► Errors that result from miscommunication
- ► Lowered productivity when managers do not motivate subordinates by communicating
- ► Increased employee turnover brought on by inadequate manager-subordinate communication

Common communication problems

We all have a hard time spotting the problems in our own communication styles. There are, however, several common weaknesses that many managers share. Perhaps you can spot some of your personal problem areas here.

Hearing only what you expect to hear

When dealing with the day-to-day aspects of a job, it is too easy to assume you've heard it all. When one of your employees or a coworker is speaking to you, you may simply nod your head with a knowing smile. You think you know what they're going to say next.

Alternatively, you may consciously (or unconsciously) ignore information that you didn't expect to hear. The classic example of this is the standard greeting, "How are you?" How often have you really listened to the answer instead of expecting the response to be "fine."

Here are some other common questions you may ask your employees without really listening to their responses:

"How's it going?"

"How was your weekend?"

"Having a busy day?"

"What did you think of _____?"

What do you think happens when you assume you already know what your employees have to say? They start giving you the canned answers you expect. They know you're not going to listen to what they say anyway. So you'll hear something like:

"How's it going?"

"Fine."

"No problems?"

"No."

"Great. Keep up the good work."

"Sure."

You go back to your office thinking you're a great communicator.

But one day, someone tells you you're a poor communicator. "What!" you explode. "I talk to my employees every day! We've got a great relationship."

Or one of your best employees suddenly gives notice. You had no idea this person was unhappy. Every day when you asked, "How are things going?" you would receive as a reply, "Fine."

What's going on?

You have to stop trying to second-guess the people who work for you and start listening. There's nothing more unmotivating to an employee than to feel that no one is listening. Your employees don't want to be paid ear-service by a preoccupied, self-centered manager.

Letting biases interfere

It's unfortunate, but biases exist in every aspect of our on-the-job relationships. If you like somebody, you're more likely to listen to what he or she has to say than if you dislike a person. In fact, even negative information is more readily accepted from those we like and respect.

Biases also affect the way we view the information we're being given. Would you pay close attention to a marginal employee who wants to discuss reworking a technical aspect of the company's procedures?

Nobody is completely unbiased. We each have our own quirks, our individual likes and dislikes. These attitudes developed during childhood, adolescence, or young adulthood. Fortunately, you don't have to be the victim of your biases. Try the following:

> ► Become aware of your feelings. Ask yourself how your background — age, sex, race, ethnicity — might be affecting your perceptions of people who are different from you.

> ► Minimize differences by understanding and accepting them. Look for a common ground from which you can form the basis for good communication. Take the time to find out what the other person's expectations are and adjust your approach to suit the situation.

> ► Find out how your behavior is influencing others. Be up-front. If you're having a hard time communicating with someone in your department, tell them you're having problems.

> ► Recognize that biases can go beyond stereotypes. One bad experience with an employee can color your future relationship —

if you let it. Remember, first impressions do count, as do second and third impressions.

▶ Be aware that your actions and attitudes can also create a biased image in the eyes of your employees. Are you aware of the image you project and the effect that image has on your relationship with your employees?

Semantics

The English language is very difficult to learn because of the great number of words with similar meanings. Even native English speakers can experience misunderstandings.

What do the phrases, "He's got a good track record," and "I couldn't get to first base" mean to you? What might these same phrases mean to an athletics coach?

The business world is full of sports and armed-service expressions. Traditionally, experiences in sports and the armed services have been primarily male experiences. When business speech is peppered with phrases from these two arenas, it can be confusing, sometimes even misleading to those, particularly women, who don't share that background. In addition, each type of business has its own language. Your attempts to communicate effectively with your employees can be severely hampered if you're using language that they don't understand.

Noise

Noise can be internal or external. It's a major factor contributing to poor communication. Since we process information much faster than we deliver information, it's easy to let our minds wander. This is even more likely to happen as we're bombarded on all sides by competing noise.

There are times when your employees need your undivided attention. At times like these you need to do everything possible to eliminate all competing noise. You should have your calls held, put up the Do Not Disturb sign — even leave the building, if necessary.

Emotions

Our moods also determine how well we listen. If we're relaxed, we'll absorb more. If we've had a rough day, we may not pay close attention to those around us.

As we've seen, honesty is often the best way to approach the people you deal with. Let them know when it's not a good time to talk to you. Be polite, but be firm. If it's not a good time, make an appointment for later.

Non-verbal communication

Many managers fail to take into consideration the importance of non-verbal communication. In fact, non-verbal cues are an important part of human communication. If we don't pay attention to body language, we may not get the full message. Poor interpretation of non-verbal messages can cause many problems. Consider the following example.

An 11th-century Scandinavian story tells of a debate that took place between a one-eyed Viking and a holy man. Each communicated only with gestures. At one point in the silent debate the holy man raised a single finger. The Viking responded by raising two fingers. The holy man then replied with three raised fingers. At this, the Viking raised a fist and the debate ended.

A spectator asked the holy man to explain what the gestures had meant. "I raised one finger," he responded, "to indicate that God is one. My opponent disputed me by displaying two fingers to show that besides God the Father, there is also God the Son. To let him know that his theology was incomplete I raised three fingers because there is a Godly Trinity: Father, Son, and Holy Spirit. But this man is a fine debater. When he made a fist to show that the Trinity is one in God, I could not argue any further."

When the Viking was asked for his version of the debate he said, "It had nothing at all to do with God. When my opponent raised one finger, he was mocking me because I have only one eye. I countered with two fingers to indicate that my one eye is the equal of his two. He continued to laugh at me by raising three fingers to show that between us we have only three eyes. I then raised a fist to let him know what he could expect if he persisted in mocking me."

The spoken word is a major mode of communication, yet it is by no means the only one. Non-verbal communication also plays a vital role in our interactions with others. Some of the most common types of non-verbal behavior are familiar to us all. A nod of the head, a wave of the hand, a frown; any of these behaviors will convey a message.

We use our entire bodies when we speak. Some people gesture a great deal. Others give different messages because of the rigidity of their bodies.

Here are a few tips to help you improve your non-verbal communication skills:

➤ It's very difficult to read somebody you don't know well. You need to be familiar with their typical reactions. Get to know your staff members and pay attention to their body language.

➤ It's helpful to know the background of a situation. What has just happened? What would your reaction be? Some facial expressions are very close, such as the expressions for fear and surprise. We may make incorrect assumptions unless we are aware of the situation.

➤ Since emotions are very fleeting, you must be able to pick up very rapid expressions. Keep in mind that many facial expressions are blends of two or more feelings.

➤ When possible, check your interpretations of non-verbal cues. This can help avoid misunderstandings.

Organizational barriers to effective communication

Over time, organizations develop very predictable patterns of communication. Many of these communication patterns are poor. Poor communication occurs because of three major problem areas:

1) *Overload:* How many pieces of paper cross your desk each day? How many memos, letters, reports, and journals? How many people stop by to ask you questions, to provide you with information, or to chat? The situation is just as bad for the people who work for you. Consider the many different kinds of messages you give to your employees each day — some verbal, some written, some non-verbal, and many conflicting. Consider the messages they're also getting from others in your organization. Is it any wonder they have a difficult time piecing all of the information together?

2) *Using the wrong medium:* Have you ever made a verbal request that was never acted upon? Have you ever committed something to paper you later realized would have been better handled in person? Have you ever called a meeting and found that

you ended up wasting the time of two or more key people? The medium is as important as the message in the business world. Often, the medium dictates whether the message is heard, understood, and acted upon. In communicating praise, for instance, a verbal "good job" is effective. A written letter of commendation may be even more effective. A verbal public acknowledgment may be the most effective of all.

3) *Failure to close:* In sales, the goal of the salesperson is to close the sale — to ask for the order. In short, to receive positive feedback. In communicating with our employees, we often fail to close the conversation. We call a meeting and never make a decision about who is going to do what. If we do make assignments, we don't follow up to see how our employees are progressing. If we find out that progress is being made, we often fail to provide the positive feedback. We fail to close. The result? Miscommunication.

A three-step approach to avoiding miscommunication

There is probably no more important (and more often overlooked) key to effective performance in the business world than good communication skills. But even in an atmosphere of cooperation, messages can be misunderstood and problems can develop. Following is a three-step approach to avoiding miscommunication.

Step 1: Verification

People very often do not wait until they have all the information they need before forming an opinion. In conversation, especially, we're often thinking ahead, because we can listen at a much faster rate than we can speak.

Verification takes place whether you're giving or receiving a message and involves very basic questions. Here are some examples.

When receiving:

"So you're saying that..."

"I hear you saying... "

"Let me make sure I understand you."

When giving:

"I want to make sure you understand what I mean. Could you tell me how you interpreted what I just said?"

In both cases, you want to verify that the communication has been accurately perceived. At first, it may seem somewhat awkward to be asking these questions. Once you have done it for a while, however, you will find that it comes more naturally. The value of avoiding problems and complications in the future far outweighs a little initial discomfort.

Step 2: Clarification

This stage involves questioning the information you're receiving and explaining the information you're giving. It's the natural follow-up to stage one, especially in those instances in which the message being sent is not being clearly understood.

Many of us are hesitant to ask too many questions for fear that we'll appear stupid. Consider how much more stupid you'll appear if you do something incorrectly or take the wrong action because you failed to clarify in the first place.

When you're giving information, be aware of this natural hesitance. Encourage the other person to ask questions so that you know you're getting your point across accurately.

At the end of any discussion, make sure that both you and the other party (or parties) understand what should happen next, if anything, or what decisions have been made. By taking extra steps to make things clear, you can avoid misunderstandings later.

Step 3: Follow-up

Have you ever attended a meeting where it seemed that everything was going quite well, good decisions were being made, and discussion about steps to take in the future seemed clear and understood — but, after the meeting, there was never any follow-up and nothing really developed from the discussion? That's what often happens with our conversations. We make some decisions, identify a course of action to pursue, but never follow up. This is a critical area that you can learn to control.

For instance, following a meeting on budget preparation, you might sum up as follows: "Okay, now, June, you'll be gathering figures on XYZ and will have them prepared by December 1. Jack, you'll be looking into ABC and will have a report to me by November 15. We'll be meeting again on December 15 to wrap this up. Any questions?"

At the clarification stage, set a time to follow up on the discussion if follow-up is appropriate. Then do it.

Here are some additional tips to help you avoid miscommunication:

➤ Avoid making such comments as "you don't understand" during the clarification stage. Such statements can result in defensive reactions. Instead you could say something like, "I don't think I'm making myself clear. What I meant is...."

➤ Don't let personal biases interfere with your ability to listen. Recognize that an attractive, charming person or somebody you personally like will be easier for you to understand than someone you find difficult to listen to because of their physical appearance, speaking ability, or your negative feelings toward them. In cases where you realize you may be biased against a person, make an extra effort to stay alert.

➤ Avoid daydreaming. Because we can listen at a rate of 400 to 600 words per minute, but speak at fewer than 200 words per minute, there is a great tendency to let our minds wander when someone is speaking to us. Instead, make a special effort to listen to what's being said.

➤ Use "I" messages when giving criticism. Take responsibility rather than trying to place blame (even inadvertently) on the other person. For instance, "I feel confused" is better than "You're confusing me."

Encouraging two-way communication

As a manager, you want to make sure that you're clearly and regularly communicating with employees. But top-down communication is only one part of the communication process. You also need to establish opportunities for bottom-up communication and encourage a culture in which employees feel comfortable sharing their ideas, perceptions, and even complaints with you.

Suggestion programs. Intranet forums. E-mail. Voice mail. Town hall meetings. The names may change, but the tools remain the same — and they proliferate at companies large and small. There is, typically, no shortage of tools to convey corporate messages to employees. But, even with so many tools, are organizations really communicating? In many cases they're not. Management sends messages down to employees. Employees attempt to send messages back up to management. Unfortunately, all too often, those messages are not part of a dialogue, but part of the growing communication clutter that exists at many companies.

It's not enough to have the tools. It's not enough to craft messages that support company goals and share those goals with employees. It's not enough to offer feedback mechanisms.

What, then, is required to encourage employees to provide honest and appropriate feedback? How can you encourage employees to engage in meaningful discussion with your company?

Desire. Employees need to believe they have something of value to say — something that's relative to the organizational goals and mission.

Opportunity. This is where the tools come in. But, in addition to the tools that technology makes available, employees also need opportunity for face-to-face feedback.

Trust. Without a climate of trust, employees are highly unlikely to share their thoughts and ideas. In an era of downsizing, reorganization, mergers, and acquisitions, employees are often afraid to say what they think.

Ensure that all the pieces of your communication efforts are working effectively by monitoring and measuring employee opinions and attitudes.

Anne Pasley-Stuart of Pasley-Stuart HR Consultants in Boise, Idaho, says, "Employees need to be cognizant of both the formal and informal channels of communication." Formal channels may include suggestion programs, intranet forums or feedback forms; informal channels may include staff meetings and other face-to-face interactions. "Management also needs to be walking around," she says, "that's one of the most critical channels for gathering information."

Removing the risk

Employees may not always be willing to share their opinions directly, however. Even in the most open cultures, there may be employees who have good ideas but are, for whatever reasons, hesitant to share them openly.

Peter Lilienthal is president of InTouch Management Communication Systems, Inc., a company in Minneapolis that provides a unique service for gathering feedback from employees who may choose to remain anonymous. Lilienthal has learned through surveys done by his organization that while 90 percent of employees believe that they have good ideas for improving the effectiveness of the companies for which they work, only about 50 percent of them say they ever share those ideas. Why?

1) There wasn't a good way.

2) They didn't think management cared.

With InTouch, employees are provided with a telephone number and passcode that they can use to access a voicemail system where they can provide feedback to management. InTouch staff members transcribe the messages, removing any identifying information, and send regular reports to the company. "You've got to make it easy for employees to provide feedback," Lilienthal says. And you have to make it safe. "Employees are perfectly willing to volunteer information, but in many cases they've either had their ideas rejected by somebody, or they're uncomfortable because they feel it might be perceived as controversial."

Actions speak louder than words. How your organization responds to employee feedback will directly influence the type of feedback you receive. If employees learn that even their most critical comments will be responded to promptly, honestly, and without rancor, they will begin to trust. If the opposite occurs — if their feedback is ignored, if the organization's responses are superficial, or if they experience, or feel that others have experienced, any type of retribution — they will not feel free to provide honest feedback or information.

How can you effectively encourage two-way communication in your organization? The answer is simple. By talking to employees and by listening sincerely to their answers.

Responding to constructive feedback

"I don't make enough money." "I want to work more flexible hours." "You're not giving me enough time to meet these deadlines." It's one thing to say, "I'm open to feedback," or, "I want my employees to share their ideas and concerns with me." It's quite another to respond effectively to those concerns. The following guidelines can help you respond effectively to employee feedback:

1) Be alert. Don't expect your employees to automatically come to you when they have a complaint. Being alert involves more than keeping your ears open. It involves keeping your eyes open as well. As one savvy manager remarked, "When I notice people starting to congregate in new clusters — hanging around with different people — I start to wonder if something's up.

2) Be a part of the company grapevine. Being part of the grapevine doesn't mean that you'll be starting or spreading rumors. It does mean that you'll make an effort to observe and listen to what employees are saying and doing, and to do what you can to correct any misperceptions or inaccuracies that are growing on the grapevine. Don't limit your activities to monitoring employees in your own department. As much as possible, stay involved at all levels and in all areas of the organization.

3) Throw out trial balloons. Trial balloons are little statements that you make to employees in an effort to get feedback on new ideas and specific situations. Here's an example of how this might work: You've heard that some of your employees are frustrated with the job-posting system — they don't feel that internal candidates are given enough of an edge. You ask an employee: "Did you see the new posting for the XYZ job? Do you think any internal candidates will apply?" or, "I think Joe would be good in the XYZ position. Do you think he'll go for it?" These kinds of casual statements, whether or not you already know what the response will be, can pave the way for a more lengthy conversation in which you'll be able to pick up on how your employees feel about specific issues.

4) Recognize early warning signs. A normally friendly employee avoids making eye contact with you as you pass each other in the hall. You enter a room and your employees suddenly grow silent or uncomfortable. Deadlines are missed. Absenteeism and tardiness increases. These are signs that a bad situation is developing.

5) Intervene at an early stage. Don't take the common attitude that, "If I ignore it, it will go away." It won't. It can be uncomfortable to take the initiative and you may feel as though you are asking for trouble. But you'll be far better off if you confront an

employee early than if you wait until the situation deteriorates even further. And you may even find that a problem employee's behavior is meant, in part, as a way of seeking your attention.

6) Hear them out. When an employee comes to you with a complaint, regardless of whether or not you feel it is valid, you owe it to them to listen. Sometimes all your employees need is the opportunity to vent. While you may not agree with their viewpoints, it's important that you demonstrate a willingness to listen objectively to what they have to say. Don't interrupt and don't make quick judgments. Just get the facts and allow employees to air their feelings. And remember to listen to what's not being said as well as what is being said. Sometimes it's the nonverbal cues that are most telling.

7) Make sure you're getting to the root of the problem. Sometimes managers will throw solutions at a problem without really examining the causal factors. If you don't really know what the problem is, you can't solve it. Make sure that you've gathered enough information to make an informed decision about what needs to be done.

8) Act. Once you've learned what's troubling your employees, the next step is to respond to their concerns. This response could mean a change in procedure, workload, or responsibilities. It could also mean simply an acknowledgment of their feelings and an explanation of why a certain procedure exists.

9) Keep your word. If you tell your employees that you're going to do something, do it, and do it in a timely manner. If your staff learns that they can rely on you to address their concerns quickly and effectively, they'll come to you first.

10) Be supportive. Understand and live by one of the cardinal rules of management: If your employees do something right, it's their success; if they do something wrong, it's a problem you both share. Don't abandon your employees when they need you the most.

11) Set a good example. You are a role model for your employees. If you drag yourself into the office every day, hole up in your office, act lethargic or grouchy, they're not likely to approach their own tasks with much energy or enthusiasm.

Communication vehicles

Whether your organization is large or small, it can sometimes become cumbersome to get news out to the people who need it when they need it. Following are some suggested communication vehicles that can help keep your staff informed:

Rap sessions

Do you ever get the feeling that all the people around you want to do is gripe? Maybe you need to set up some form of regular rap session. They may need a way to air their grievances. Especially in the rank and file, opportunities for airing opinions, expressing concerns, or voicing displeasure are limited. These employees are not allowed the input granted to upper or even middle management. Sometimes all they really need is a chance to get together and rap. Rap sessions can be either formal (structured) or informal (unstructured). The type you choose will depend on the climate of your organization.

If you're aware of a great deal of employee hostility, you might decide to use a structured form of rap session. You should select a chairperson, schedule regular meetings with specific topics of discussion for the agenda, and be certain to have representatives of management present at these sessions.

If, however, the climate of your organization is relatively peaceful, unstructured rap sessions may work wonderfully. You might still suggest topics of discussion and have management representation, but these sessions would need less monitoring and less control.

Regular meetings

Meetings are sometimes cursed, yet they are a vital part of the formal communication structure. Regular department meetings in addition to regular meetings with individual department members should be part of your communication improvement program. These meetings are a perfect time to discuss the issues of rules and policies, current organizational activities, past results, and future plans.

Grievance or suggestion system

Certainly you should encourage employees to express concerns and complaints directly to their managers. However, you should also realize that there will be times when an employee simply will not feel comfortable talking to his or her immediate manager. That's why you need a formal grievance procedure. That's also why you may need a suggestion box. Granted, some of the anonymous complaints you get may seem vicious and non-constructive. Behind every vicious complaint, though, is an unhappy employee. And unhappy employees can spread discontent.

Never dismiss a complaint, regardless of how insignificant you think it might be. If you do, you risk —

- ➤ having employees feel that you don't care what they think,
- ➤ letting a small problem become a big problem that could take months to solve, and
- ➤ creating misunderstandings that you could have resolved.

For your suggestion system to work, you must let employees know what suggestions you have received and what action you intend to take. Many companies also establish reward systems for particularly useful suggestions.

Intranet forums

Technology has allowed companies to simplify many processes — including communications. Consider how your company's intranet or e-mail system could help improve communication within your organization. While some managers may be hesitant to allow employees to express their opinions (sometimes negative opinions) in a public forum, keep in mind that access to on-line communication channels does not create the issues that employees raise. Those issues were already there — you just may not have known about them. If messages in on-line forums and e-mail communication are pervasively negative and mean-spirited, it may be symptomatic of other issues.

Open channels of communication naturally lend themselves to both positive and negative messages, so you must expect to be the target of criticism. The way in which you respond to this form of open communication will impact the tone, frequency, and content of future messages, particularly if your response is also made public. A well-reasoned, non-defensive, on-line response to a negative employee message can send a very positive signal about your willingness to listen to employees and your ability to take an objective stance. It's not easy to remain objective and to respond calmly to negative feedback from employees — especially when that feedback is presented in an immature or disrespectful manner. But your level-headed response speaks volumes and sets the stage for future interactions.

When responding to negative feedback:

► Manage your initial reaction. It is natural to feel defensive when you or your department is the target of negative feedback, but resist the impulse to blast back with an equally negative response.

► Recognize that the sender of the message is coming from a different frame of reference. He or she doesn't know what you know or have all of the background information.

► Consider that you are actually lucky to know about these negative feelings. Without the benefit of the open forum, you might not be aware of negative information or frustrations related to your department that are, nevertheless, being shared throughout the organization.

► Be honest. As in media relations, the phrase "Tell it all and tell it now" is good advice. Thank the sender for the feedback. Apologize if necessary. Provide background. Explain, but don't be defensive.

Open-door policies

Technology is wonderful, but it can also be a barrier between you and your employees. Remember that face to face is the most effective means of communication. Don't hide behind e-mail messages and forum conversations.

Being available to your employees and letting them know that you are available is half the battle in developing good communications. Having an open-door policy, though, means more than having your door open. It means being ready to listen when your employees come to you with suggestions, problems, or complaints.

When you make yourself available to your subordinates, you are emphasizing supportiveness, receptivity, and participation. You increase the likelihood that the information your employees receive is accurate information, and you increase motivation.

Naturally, you won't accept or use every idea or suggestion that comes your way. The fact that you are there to listen with an open mind means a great deal. Your employees don't want to hear, "We tried that before and it didn't work." On the other hand, they don't have to hear, "That's a wonderful idea. We'll do it immediately." They should hear, "Thank you for the suggestion. I appreciate every comment you make because it lets me know how concerned you are with the company and that's important. You matter. You're important."

There are also benefits to you in having an open-door policy:

- ▶ You will be privy to what's going on in the rank and file. You will become part of the grapevine, a very powerful position to be in.

- ▶ You will know about minor problems before they become big ones, so you can begin corrective action immediately.

- ▶ You will be able to encourage a team spirit among your employees. You will be influencing them directly — not merely in an advisory capacity.

An open door does not mean that you can be interrupted any time. It may mean that you can be seen by appointment only. It may mean that you're available during certain times of the day. It is important, however, that you aren't frequently unavailable or too busy to be approached.

Opinion surveys

Don't just sit around wondering what your employees have on their minds. Ask them. Employee surveys are a quick, effective means of gathering information from employees in every area of the company. You won't be able to know who said what, but you will be able to get a good, overall feel for company-wide attitudes and perceptions.

Two important points need to be made here:

- ▶ Don't conduct opinion surveys too often. It reduces their effectiveness and may make employees think you don't know what you're doing.

- ▶ Share the results with your employees.

Social gatherings

Special events and company-sponsored parties are good ways to open up communication channels. The relaxed atmosphere at these gatherings makes them a good place for a free exchange of casual information. At social gatherings, you are able to do the following:

▶ Get to know employees and their families more personally. Understanding the personal aspects of your employees' lives can help you understand their goals, aspirations, and motivations.

▶ Observe the casual interactions among employees. Who speaks to whom? Often, these casual friendships give you clues to the informal communication network of your organization.

▶ Relate non-defensively to problem employees. Social events can sometimes provide you with just the opportunity to get closer to a difficult worker.

Never underestimate the power or value of the organizational grapevine. And never try to stop it. For one thing, you can't. For another, the grapevine is a vital form of informal communication. In fact, studies have shown that the information carried through the grapevine is approximately 80 percent accurate. If you're not already a part of the grapevine, you should make an attempt to become a part of it.

Creative communication: Lessons from the front lines

What are companies doing to improve communication among their ranks? Plenty. The following are some examples of actual communication practices from companies in a variety of industries.

At Fenwick & West LLP, a law firm that was on *Fortune Magazine*'s list of "100 Best Places to Work in America," every administrative manager is responsible for preparing a regular newsletter to inform employees about the activities, accomplishments, and plans of his or her department. The newsletters are informal and upbeat. The firm also has an anonymous e-mail system that allows anyone in the firm to send a message to management without being identified. The system is rarely used, however. Why? Because employees recognize the culture of openness that exists in the firm and are confident that management is willing to listen and respond to their concerns.

At G.E. Capital, manager's toolkits are used to help managers communicate effectively with their staff members. The toolkits provide managers with simple tools that they can use to plan communication activities, measure communication results, and ensure that the messages from the top of the organization are clearly translated and communicated to staff members. Workshops are also provided to ensure that managers have the training they need to be effective communicators.

At Continental Airlines, every year since 1995, a simple, 10-question leadership communication survey has been sent out to monitor the effectiveness of managers' communications. Managers are held accountable for the results, which are considered part of their annual evaluations.

FedEx has an internal private business television network (FXTV), which is used to facilitate communications to its large employee population. The FXTV network includes more than 1,000 satellite connections in the U.S., Canada, and Europe. The network allows the company to air live telecasts that include phone-in question-and-answer sessions between corporate officers and employees on a variety of topics.

SAIC is one of the largest majority employee-owned firms in the world. A high technology company, SAIC has more than $5 billion in revenue and more than 40,000 employees in 150 cities worldwide. To communicate with employees, SAIC has a very active intranet web set called EON (the Employee Owner's Network), which includes information on how to become an owner, what it means to become an owner, as well as employee testimonials and numerous related articles. Employees are also able to track the value of company stock (which is not publicly traded) on the site. The site also allows the opportunity for employees to ask questions and give feedback.

At KPMG, LLP, a consulting firm, face-to-face meetings are used to allow for two-way feedback and discussion. And, because all employees aren't able to attend these open forums, summaries of the Q&A at each meeting are gathered, organized by topic, and attached to the firm's weekly electronic newsletter, *InfoTrack*.

At 3M, employees are able to take advantage of the "Between Us" program, a confidential way to submit comments to the company's leaders on sensitive subjects about which they wish to remain anonymous. Employees submit questions to executives and are able to specify from whom they would like to receive a response — if they don't know, the communication department directs the question to the appropriate place.

When Larry Weinbach joined Unisys in 1997 as the company's leader, he opened up the communication channels by encouraging employees to send him e-mails directly. They did. He received 4000 e-mail messages during his first few months with Unisys, and he responded directly to each one. The symbolism of what he did had an impact on the culture, letting employees know that they had an opportunity to be heard — and the right to expect a response.

At Brobeck, Phleger & Harrison, LLP, a San Francisco law firm, brown-bag lunches are offered each month where staff members are hosted by the firm's chairman, firm-wide managing partner, and executive director. The lunch is intended to encourage a free exchange of ideas between staff and upper management, and is video-conferenced to all of the firm's offices. During the meetings, the firm's management updates staff on the strategic direction of the firm and other issues, including sensitive financial information. Staff members are encouraged to talk openly about any concerns.

At Eastman Kodak, it's not unusual for a small group of employees to be called together to offer insights and feedback on communication initiatives — before they're rolled out. Employees are trusted to maintain the confidentiality of information they might receive, and their comments are used to improve the way these messages are conveyed throughout the organization. Because employees are trusted, they are more likely to trust management.

Part III

Part III

Part III: Programs, Polices, and Practices

Employers are doing more than ever before to find unique ways to motivate and reward employees. In fact, studies indicate that employers in the 21st century are more frequently turning to non-monetary rewards. Watson Wyatt's fifth annual Strategic Rewards® survey conducted in 2000, which studied 410 employers, indicated that the three most prevalent non-monetary rewards were advancement opportunities (76 percent — up from 60 percent in 1999), flexible work schedules (73 percent, up from 64 percent), and opportunities to learn new skills (68 percent, up from 62 percent).

Employers participating in the survey were asked to identify their top performers and invite them to participate in a survey to measure and rank their opinions about the effectiveness of various reward programs. Among workers under 30, the following were the five highest-scoring items:

- ► Opportunity to develop skills
- ► Opportunity for promotion
- ► Compensation
- ► Vacation/paid time off

- Type of people/culture

The study also noted that, not surprisingly, employees in different demographic groups had different preferences, supporting the need to build flexibility into benefit and reward structures. However, the opportunity to develop skills was consistently rated as a top-five factor across the board, supporting a move toward more focus on non-monetary rewards.

Brobeck, Phleger & Harrison, LLP is a law firm in San Francisco — one of four law firms named in *Fortune Magazine*'s 2000 list of "100 Best Companies to Work For." This company has found, first-hand, that a combination of monetary and non-monetary incentives can yield positive results. Brobeck is dedicated to providing a non-hierarchical work environment, a collegial atmosphere, and an array of perks and benefits that "bring out the best in people, both personally and professionally," says Tower C. Snow, Jr., Brobeck's chairman. The firm offers both monetary and non-monetary benefits to its associates, including the following:

- Upward review. Partners and supervising attorneys are subject to a thorough review by associates once a year. Low-scoring partners are given executive coaches for their personal development and to help them improve in the areas identified in the survey.

- A $1000 bonus on Valentine's Day. All Brobeck non-attorneys receive the bonus and the firm pays all withholding taxes, meaning the check each individual receives totals exactly $1000.

- Business casual dress. Dress is business casual every day of the year in every office.

- Stock investment funds for every individual in the firm. Brobeck was the first law firm in the country to have a stock investment fund for its non-attorneys — not just for its associates and partners.

- Home-loan assistance program. Brobeck provides a guaranty on a portion of a first mortgage on all associates' primary residences, when the loan amount is between 80 percent and 95 percent of the value of the home.

- Suggestion box. All staff and non-partner attorneys are encouraged to make suggestions on enhancing the work environment, increasing productivity, or any other ideas to improve the firm, and the best ideas receive a $1000 award.

- ▶ Brobeck STAR Award. This program visibly expresses the firm's appreciation to members of its administrative staff who, through their dedication and resourcefulness, make especially meaningful contributions to the improved operation of the firm. Each month, one winner is announced at the staff brown-bag lunch and is presented with a $150 gift certificate for dinner as well as a crystal star from Tiffany & Co. At the end of the year, the 12 winners are entered into a drawing for a $1000 "Weekend on the Firm."

While managers are the first line of influence for motivating employees, managers must operate within an environment that is driven by organizational programs, policies, and practices. Sometimes managers are hampered by these practices because they are not conducive to meeting the needs of today's employees. However, even though managers may not be involved in setting policy, they are in a position to influence an organization's policy, whether through serving on task forces and committees, or simply by providing information and insights.

This section takes a look at a variety of organizational policies, practices, and procedures that have an influence on employee motivation and job satisfaction.

7
BENEFITS

BMC software is a leading provider of e-business systems management. If you think tuition reimbursement and a great vacation package represent good benefits, think again. Think about an afternoon massage and a game of bocci ball, on-site hair salons and gifts for mothers and fathers to be. BMC offers employees all of these benefits and more, including:

- ► paid time off for community service (up to five days);

- ► a scholarship fund — four $10,000 scholarships awarded each year to children of BMC employees;

- ► company-paid assistance for employees who want to quit smoking;

- ► massage therapy, hair salon, manicures, and pedicures;

- ► basketball court, horseshoe, bocci ball, outdoor sand volleyball, putting green;

- ► personal concierge services (car repair, gifts, etc.);

- ► parenting seminars; and

➤ child-care/adoption/elder-care resource and referral services.

In the next few years, employees will judge their employers not just on how many vacation days they get, but on whether their companies give them access to discounted airline tickets to make those days off even more valuable, according to RewardsPlus (www.rewardsplus.com), a Web-based benefits firm. And, they say, it won't be too long before employees demand such benefits as financial planning, massage therapy, retail discounts, and acupuncture treatments in addition to the traditional health care and 401(k) plans.

The types of benefits being offered to employees in the 21st century are changing rapidly: pet insurance, legal services, auto insurance, laptops, and high-speed Internet access are just a few of the benefits that companies can now make available to employees. In fact, RewardsPlus predicts that benefits in the future will be tailored to individual employee needs, blurring the distinction between what have traditionally been considered core and voluntary benefits. Some of the unique benefits that RewardsPlus predict will become increasingly prevalent include the following:

➤ Portable retirement plans

➤ Coverage for alternative medicine such as acupuncture, herbal remedies, and massage therapy

➤ Elder care

➤ Child-care programs (on-site and off-site assistance)

➤ Laser eye surgery

➤ Discounted airline/hotel fares/vacation plans

➤ Entertainment discounts

➤ Online bill payment

➤ Paternity benefits

➤ Home office/telecommuting tools

➤ Long-term care

➤ Online and offline retailer discounts

Offering a variety of benefits and options to employees is important in this age of diversity. The workforce is comprised of individuals from a wide range of age groups and educational backgrounds, with a wide variation of individual needs. Consider the following examples:

Janelle is 18, not very concerned about her retirement, but wishing she had more than one week of vacation to use. Unused to the 9-to-5 lifestyle, a week off just doesn't seem like much time.

Doug is 58 and concerned about the future needs of himself and his wife as they approach retirement. He wishes his company would offer some form of retirement savings plan that would allow him to contribute a portion of his income on a tax-deferred basis and perhaps offer a reciprocal contribution from the company as well.

Sandy is 35 and a single mother of two. Not only is daycare expensive and eating up her limited disposable income, but she finds it difficult to be away from her children all day. She thinks it would be great if her company offered daycare benefits of some sort.

Bob is 42 and married with four children, and his wife is pregnant. His most fervent wish? That his company would offer a more generous healthcare program. His medical and dental expenses are crippling him, and he'd gladly trade in a couple of weeks of vacation time for more extensive health coverage.

Meeting the needs of a diverse workforce through flexible benefits

Janelle, Doug, Sandy, and Bob are all good examples of the employee of the 21st century. They demonstrate that packaged benefit programs simply don't meet the needs of employees who make up today's very diverse workforce.

We've already seen that employees are uniquely motivated. They're also unique in their need for various employee benefits.

Vacation, sick pay, and health insurance are often considered standard benefits. Most companies have policies in place for how these benefits are distributed — it usually works something like this: one week of paid vacation after one full year of employment, eligible for health plan immediately; choice between individual plan (completely paid by company) or family plan (company pays 50 percent).

The standard policy serves a purpose, but it's as futile to apply the same benefit strategies to all employees as it is to apply the same motivational strategies.

Businesses have historically designed their benefit programs for the traditional family, in which Dad goes to work every day and Mom stays home to care for the children. But, as we all know, this traditional family no longer exists.

Enter flexible spending accounts, or FSAs, which have gained widespread acceptance at large corporations since the accounts were first created by the Revenue Act of 1978. Also referred to as cafeteria plans (because employees may pick and choose from a variety of options, spending their "flex dollars" based on their unique individual needs), these plans not only serve the individual needs of employees but, in many cases, save money for the employer as well.

Because of this, more companies are offering flexible benefit plans that provide employees with a certain number of benefit dollars that they can spend on a variety of benefit options that may include health and dental insurance, vacation time, and even dependent care. Employees may also allocate a certain amount of each paycheck, before taxes, to be used to pay for healthcare or child-care expenses.

For example, Dan is widowed and supporting two pre-school children. In the past, he has paid for child care with money he receives each week from his check — his take-home pay, or taxable income. This money has already been reduced by deductions for state and federal income tax and Social Security tax. Through his company's flexible benefit program he is able to choose child care from the benefits offered. The flexible compensation dollars he spends for child care are not included in his gross income. Therefore, this amount is not taxed. The tax saving Dan realizes can mean a significant increase in his take-home pay.

As you can see, the major advantage of these flexible benefit programs is the ability to meet individual needs — and, as we've already discussed, meeting individual needs is what motivating employees is all about.

While flexible spending accounts were originally used primarily by very large companies that could afford to hire outside agencies to assist with administration of the program, recent developments in the marketplace have made FSAs easier than ever to offer. FSAs have become streamlined and much easier to oversee, meaning that many small firms can offer these programs with the aid of a bookkeeper and a software program.

Determining which benefits to include in a flexible benefit plan may at first seem to be a major task. For many companies, however, it has involved no more than a brief survey to determine which benefits employees are most likely to take advantage of. The results of such a survey allow management to determine the best way to set up the program. Obviously, before starting a flexible benefits plan, a company must determine whether expected savings will offset the costs. Most companies feel that these programs are cost effective.

Another important factor in establishing a successful flexible benefit program is employee understanding. The options available and tax implications involved can be confusing. If employees do not understand the plan, they will not make use of it. Then, neither the employee nor the employer will save anything in the process.

The big benefit of these plans is flexibility. Companies large and small are finding that it's difficult to attract, retain, or motivate employees with the traditional benefit structure of vacation and healthcare. Employees have varying needs and appreciate greater flexibility in meeting those needs. Flexible benefit plans can provide that flexibility.

Addressing employee work/life needs

A 2000 online survey by SurveySite on "Balancing Work and Life" revealed that 60 percent of the 1862 respondents felt it was difficult to be professionally successful as well highly involved in their family and life relationships. A vast majority of job-seekers were looking for career opportunities with flexible work environments (87 percent).

The needs of employees have changed dramatically over the past 30 years, and their demands have grown in a tight marketplace. Employers need to stay on top of, and even ahead of, the current changes in employee attitude.

An online survey conducted by *the Washington Post's* Web site (www.washingtonpost.com) asked respondents what special privileges would be most appealing to them. Of the 3400 respondents, the results broke down as follows:

TABLE 1	
Telecommuting	548
Training/tuition	396
Flextime	379
Benefits	375
Bonus	370
Fitness	357
Money	334
Other perks	302
Time off/vacation	227
Opportunity/growth	109
Recognition/security	80

Recognizing the diverse needs of employees, more companies are offering creative services — from on-site dry cleaning to cafeteria take-home meals — to help boost employee job satisfaction and overall wellness. Businesses have learned that people-friendly and family-friendly workplaces can reduce turnover costs, relieve employee stress, and strengthen recruiting and retention efforts.

Popular wisdom used to prescribe that employees should leave their home lives at home. Today, however, there is a widespread understanding that personal issues do impact performance in the workplace, and that managers should assist employees in balancing their work and life needs.

Because of a decreasing labor pool, employers must become the "employer of choice" and shift their focus from recruitment to retention of current employees, says Anne Pasley-Stuart, president of Pasley-Stuart HR Consultants. Employee dissatisfaction with an organization can cover a lot of territory, Pasley-Stuart says, including failure of the organization to support a balance between work and personal life.

There's even a growing level of comfort in many organizations for dealing with issues of spirituality in the workplace. Martin Rutte (www.martinrutte.com), one of the co-authors of *Chicken Soup for the Soul at Work*, and president of Livelihood, a management consulting firm in Santa Fe, New Mexico, says, "Years ago we were permitted only to talk about issues of the business — profit/loss, advertising, strictly business things. Then we moved a little into the personal area when we started to talk about my career. Then we moved more into the personal area with all of the mental health and emotional issues." Rutte continues, "The very nature and meaning of what it means to be at work has changed."

Family first: A no-cost/low-cost benefit

When Working Mother first began its Best Companies award program in 1985, it struggled to find 30 employers interested in participating. Today more than 500 applications are received annually from businesses and industries of all types and sizes.

But work/life needs aren't limited to female employees. Family-friendly policies are equally applicable to males in the workplace and just as positively received. And these policies and options don't have to cost a bundle. Companies are coming up with many unique and innovative ways to address the work/life needs of their employees.

Sharon Jordan-Evans, co-author with Beverly Kaye of *Love 'Em or Lose 'Em: Getting Good People to Stay,* says that even at companies in which policies may not overtly support a family-friendly approach, there are things the manager can do to address employee work/life needs. She suggests that managers in these situations do the following:

1) Redefine the word "family." Too often, Jordan-Evans says, we define the family in terms of a traditional view — mom, dad, and two kids. In fact, families can encompass a variety of people (and pet!) combinations — "a single male caring for his aging father, a young newlywed couple with no kids, a Gen X'er and his dog — these are all families and they can feel cheated when their workplace's 'family friendly' policies leave them out." Her advice to managers: "Assume that every one of your employees is part of a family, however that's defined."

2) Get interested. Sit down with individual employees and find out what's important to them. Each employee will have different needs, Jordan-Evans stresses. She urges managers to forget

about trying to treat everybody the same. "Treat them fairly and equitably, yes. But the same? No, because we each want different things. Not everybody wants to leave at 3:00 p.m. to take their dog to a dog show. Don't assume that because you give one person flexibility in one area that everybody else will feel somehow left out."

3) Get flexible. Jordan-Evans encourages managers to be creative and to look for ways in which they can be flexible in meeting employee needs. "Instead of jumping to 'no, we can't do that because it would set a nasty precedent,' or 'the policies don't allow for that,' question the rules a bit. Much of this is up to the individual manager to use his or her budget wisely to get very creative and to be in tune to people's individual needs and wants."

Time off when they want it: PTO programs

PTO (paid time off) plans pool employees' vacation, holiday, and sick time into one pot from which they can draw for any time-off needs, including vacations, illnesses, care of family members, religious observances, marriage, funerals, community service, and other personal business that cannot be taken care of after work.

The concept not only allows flexibility for employees, but removes some of the distrust that historically exists when employees call in sick. A typical PTO plan lumps together all paid days into one bank that allows employees to take time off when they need it. Instead of having 10 vacation days, 6 sick days, and 1 personal day, the employee would have 17 PTO days to use for any personal reason.

Employees still receive advance approval from their supervisor or manager to take time off, according to the company's policies, but there is no requirement for employees to give a reason for the leave and, as a result, no need for the supervisor to serve as a watchdog in verifying whether an employee calling in sick was really sick.

Employees generally value PTO plans because of the flexibility, particularly those employees who do not have to deal with sick children or who are infrequently sick themselves. For these staff members, PTO offers extra days that formerly had to be used for sick time only.

This can present some problems, however. Since sick time and vacation time are lumped together, employees may not save time to use for illnesses that may occur later in the year, and this could result in employers granting PTO time as well as additional unpaid time off if the employee becomes ill later in the year, after the PTO days have been used.

FMLA (Family Medical Leave Act) considerations come into play here as well. Since employees are not required to tell managers why they're taking time off, the manager may not identify when an employee has a serious health condition that would be covered under FMLA.

PTO plans may or may not be appropriate for your company. Some of the things your organization would want to consider before implementing such a plan include the following:

► *Current levels of absenteeism:* If your staff includes employees who need time off for personal needs not covered by the traditional vacation/sick plan (i.e., time off to care for elderly parents or young children), a PTO play may serve these needs.

► *Culture:* In a flexible environment, PTO plans can work well. In a more controlled environment, they may not.

► *FMLA issues:* FMLA issues can be complex. Your company will want to consider how a PTO plan could increase the difficult of tracking FMLA-related absences.

► *Laws related to termination pay:* Some jurisdictions require payment of unused vacation at termination. If you're rolling sick time and holiday time into your PTO pool, and you haven't previously paid for sick or holiday time at termination, these laws could negatively impact these costs.

Addressing the work/life needs of employees doesn't necessarily have to mean a major shift in benefit structure or a major increase in salary expenses. In fact, one very important benefit to employees costs nothing at all: flexibility. Work/life issues do matter to today's employees. It's important, though, to remember that every employee has different needs. What matters to — and motivates — one employee, may not move another.

In *Love 'Em or Lose 'Em: Getting Good People to Stay,* Jordan Evans and her co-author, Beverly Kaye, offer a number of strategies and solutions for helping organizations address the work/life needs of employees:

► If employees must travel on weekends, offer something in exchange, such as compensation time during the week or allowing family members to travel with the employee.

- When your employees travel to areas where they have family or friends, allow them to spend extra time with those people at the beginning or end of the business trip.

- If company policy absolutely prohibits bringing pets to work, consider a picnic in a park where those furry family members are welcome.

- Give your employees a floating day off per year to be used for a special occasion. Or suggest they go home early on birthdays or anniversaries.

- Have a party for your team and their families. Invite the kids (or hire sitters for small ones) and go for pizza together.

- When an employee asks about working from home, really explore that possibility. What are the upsides? Downsides? Get creative about how that might work to benefit both the employee and your team.

Meeting the needs of working parents

Dual career marriages are no longer the exception — they're the rule. These dual career marriages, of course, frequently involve more than two people. Many involve children or other dependents, a complicating factor that can cause as much frustration for an employer as it can for parents.

Employers are often concerned with the following questions:

- When will a new mother (or father) return to work?

- How much time will be lost on the job due to dependent-care problems?

- What effect will worrying about a young or ailing family member have on productivity?

- How will other workers react to the special requirements of working parents and caregivers?

The questions that employees have usually involve the following concerns:

- How much time will I be able to spend at home with the new child?

- Where will I find qualified dependent care?

- What do I do when dependents are sick?

- Will my supervisor be flexible in terms of hours worked?

- What effect will my part-time parenting have on the children?

Employees are affected, first, by heightened stress caused by the increased responsibility of trying to hold down a full-time job and manage the home concurrently; and second, by concern over the shortage of quality dependent care, coupled with feelings of guilt over not spending enough time with the family. These strong feelings lead to stress, which leads to lack of productivity. As a manager, you play a key role in reducing these feelings of stress.

There are two important areas where employers are in a position to provide support and assistance to employees concerned about caring for their families: flexible scheduling — which addresses the three o'clock syndrome — and the establishment of company-subsidized or company-sponsored child care.

The three o'clock syndrome, and what you can (and should) do about it

The three o'clock syndrome refers to reduced productivity and higher error and accident rates as employees begin thinking of their children around the time school gets out. This drop in productivity, however, isn't limited to late afternoon. It can occur at any time. Let's take a look at a few examples.

> *Sam's son started kindergarten last week. Sam has been noticeably preoccupied at work and has been spending an inordinate amount of time on the phone. He needs to come in later so he can see his son off to school and needs to leave earlier so he can be there when the bus drops him off.*
>
> *Joelle's preteen son is having problems in school. She receives numerous calls from the principal each week and is often asked to come to the school.*
>
> *Jerry's daughter is in preschool, but frequently ill. He often needs to take days off work to care for her, even though he and his wife take turns with this particular responsibility.*

Illness, non-standard work schedules, teacher's conferences, school plays — these are just a few of the special circumstances in which working parents find themselves involved. Most parents hesitate to bring up their personal concerns in the work setting. They struggle through these upsets, trying their hardest to focus on their jobs. They often fail.

It is simply not possible to separate one's personal life from one's professional life. The two are inextricably intermeshed; what happens in one area can't help but affect the other.

As managers, the first step you can take to alleviate some of these difficulties is awareness. Understanding and allowing for flexible scheduling is one of the simplest and most appreciated steps you can take.

Very often it is just not possible for a working parent to maintain the hours of 8:00 a.m. to 5:00 p.m. without frequent adjustments. Children get sick. They have doctor appointments, they have days off school, and so on. Letting your employees know that you're aware of these needs will go a long way toward alleviating the stress of trying to balance responsibilities to children with responsibilities to the job.

The child-care dilemma

Flexibility isn't the only need that your employees have. Many also have concerns about how their young children will be cared for while they're at work. They are concerned both about the quality of the care and the cost.

The Society for Human Resource Management (SHRM) 2000 Benefits Survey found that only 3 percent of surveyed employers offer on-site daycare services for employees (6 percent subsidize the cost of child care and 3 percent offer daycare subsidies).

What can we do to meet the needs of our employees with children? There are three primary areas of employee child-care assistance: on-site or near-site child-care centers, child-care vouchers and financial assistance, and information and referral services.

1) *On-site or near-site child-care centers:* With this option, an employer operates a child-care facility on company premises or provides support to a nearby center. Employers may either choose to run the program themselves or rent space to a professional organization. The cost of the program may be subsidized, employees may pay based on a sliding-fee scale according to their income, or employers may simply pass along

the costs to those employees using the service. Some companies also offer a variation of these child-care services to employees with sick children — sick-child care allows employees to feel confident that their sick child is being effectively cared for, while reducing absenteeism for the employer.

2) *Child-care vouchers and financial assistance:* With a voucher system, the employer provides employees with coupons worth money toward the cost of child-care services. The coupons purchase licensed child care and allow parents to make all the decisions about child-care arrangements. Another option is including child-care benefits as part of a flexible benefits program.

3) *Information and referral:* With an information and referral system, the company offers information about child-care services to employees free of charge. Some companies contract with local information and referral agencies that maintain computerized lists of available child-care services. An I&R agency researches local facilities and publishes its findings regularly for the company's staff. Details on location, age groups, hours, and number of openings are provided.

Workers without children

But what about the needs of workers without children? Or those whose children are grown and no longer create demands on their time? Employees frequently compare benefits, identifying who receives what and making sure they are getting their fair share. Some childless employees respond negatively to the special benefits and flexibility offered to employees with children (some employers consider this backlash). The extension of flexibility to all staff members can play a critical role in minimizing feelings of inequity. In fact, while child-friendly benefits have become popular and receive a great deal of media attention, they now apply to the minority of workers.

The Bureau of Labor Statistics reports that 60 percent of employees in the workforce at any given time do not have children under the age of 18 in the household.

In addition, by 2010, the number of childless couples in the U.S. is expected to increase by 50 percent. After 2005, single people and married couples without children are expected to become the most common types of households in the country, according to the Census Bureau.

To avoid the perception of inequity, managers should take a broader approach. Some simple options might include the following:

- Find out what your employees want. Each organization will have different needs based upon the characteristics of its workforce. Take the pulse of your employees with a survey or poll.

- Implement life-friendly as opposed to family-friendly options.

- Recommend the implementation of a flexible benefit plan, allowing employees to choose those options which are most important to them.

- Institute non-explanatory requests for flexible arrangements. Rather than looking at the reason for the request (i.e., attending a child's sporting event), consider the impact of the request on the company. After all, shouldn't a childless worker be allowed the same flexibility — to take a pet to the vet, for example — as employees with children, as long as the department or company isn't negatively impacted?

Telecommuting

Jack Nilles coined the terms telecommuting and teleworking in 1973. Since that time, telecommuting has become an increasingly popular option for employees. In fact, according to a late 1997 study conducted by the William Olsten Center for Workforce Strategies, a majority of North American companies (51 percent) say that they permit employees to telecommute through ongoing or pilot programs. And, according to the International Telework Association & Council, about 20 million Americans — nearly 10 percent of working adults — now telecommute at least one day a month.

Could telecommuting be an option for your employees? You might be surprised.

Jim Miller works at U.S. West and is passionate about telecommuting and the benefits it offers to employees and the businesses they work for. His advice to any organization considering telecommuting as an option is to "answer the five Ws before you answer the one H." According to Miller, "Knowing who, what, when, where and why, tells you how." Too often, he says, companies try to figure out "how" before they clearly understand what it is they're really trying to do.

1) Who? The question of who is an important one. Not everybody is cut out to be a telecommuter. The decision will hinge on the position and on the individual. Certainly a bank teller could not do his or her job from a remote location. An accountant, though, could operate from a remote location. Ultimately, the decision of whether telecommuting is a viable work alternative would hinge on the individual's unique personal characteristics. Obviously telecommuting isn't for everyone. It takes a lot of personal discipline to work out of your home. Carol Stein operates HR Library, an Internet research company. The people who work for her are librarians with Master's degrees in library science. They're based all over the country, ranging from a woman who works from a farm in Maine to a woman who operates from her home in Kissimmee, Florida. "It works for people who have a life outside of work," Stein says. "If work is your life and you chit-chat around the coffee machine, or if your friends are always the people you work with, then telecommuting may not work for you."

2) What? There are a variety of jobs that can be successfully handled from a remote location — even managing employees. Initially, when you look at a job you may say, "There's no way that could be done at home." But keep an open mind and be creative. Focus on the work that needs to be done and the interactions that are involved in getting the work done. Could marketing communication tasks be handled off-site? Probably. Could transcriptionist duties? Certainly. Could sales duties? Probably. Could one-on-one customer interaction? Probably not. Jobs that require a lot of face-to-face contact or frequent meetings can't be done from home. But many jobs can.

3) When? Stein has organized her telecommuting staff around a core set of hours — from 8:00 a.m. to 12:00 p.m. — when they must be available to communicate either by phone or on-line. "Other than the core set of hours," she says, "I don't care when they work — all I care about is that they get their work done when they commit to getting it done. It's a very different work style. It allows the individual, including me, to work when they are at their strongest." You will need to work with the telecommuter to determine what hours make the most sense for the particular position you're dealing with. A lot will depend on the customer group — internal and external — that the telecommuter is serving.

4) Where? Telecommuting often occurs at the employee's home. But there are other options as well. A satellite office could be considered a telecommuting location. So could a neighborhood work center — a workplace that is shared by multiple businesses and that allows employees to avoid long commutes. Another option is the virtual office, an arrangement in which an employee literally has no set working place. This type of arrangement is very typical for salespeople, for example.

5) Why? Sometimes the move to telecommuting is driven by the desire to retain a valuable employee. But there are other reasons. When the Olympics were scheduled in Salt Lake City, a massive road-construction project created concern about how people were going to get to and from work. Employers began looking at various options, such as telecommuting. Space constraints can be another reason. So can the need to attract highly qualified talent that may not be available in your local market.

6) How? The answer to this question will involve both technology and communication. What kind of equipment and technology will the employee require to work from home? Can your company support those needs? What kind of communication needs will the employee have? Will he or she be required to come into the office on occasion to interact with other staff members? What about training? Both telecommuters and their managers will need to become comfortable with the unique aspects of this managerial relationship.

It can be difficult for managers to make the transition from managing people at the office to managing them at some other location. But it's really just a matter of perception. Many managers are fearful of allowing people to telecommute because they won't be able to physically see them. But consider how much of your time now is spent actually observing the work of your staff members.

Having buy-in from top management is critical to developing a successful telecommuting arrangement. So is a well developed training program. Training should be part of the telecommuting program's development from the conceptual stage. A formalized system of policies and procedures should follow. Both you and your telecommuting employees should have a good understanding of the work to be performed and the quality and quantity standards for that work, as well as an understanding of the details of the relationship — like what hours the telecommuter should be available, and who will provide the telecommuter's home equipment.

Telecommuting is destined to become even more prevalent in the years ahead. The key is to find a way to make it work for you and your employees. Whether it's an extensive program that is used throughout your organization, or a one-time trial basis designed to retain a critical employee, there are successful models in place that prove telecommuting to be a viable option.

Little things mean a lot

At Fenwick & West, LLP, a law firm that was included in *Fortune magazine*'s "100 Best Places to Work" list in 2000, a variety of benefits are offered to employees, from the traditional to the more creative.

For example, employees can save on their pets' medical bills by enrolling in pet health and accident insurance, a lactation room is offered for nursing mothers, and food is a prevalent perk. Employees are provided with four varieties of coffee, orange juice, assorted teas, hot chocolate, hot soups, and seasonal specialty items (like ice cream socials during hot, summer months, and eggnog during the winter holidays). On evenings from Monday through Thursday, the firm serves a complete dinner for all employees who are working late. New employees are warned that they could gain five, ten, even fifteen pounds during their first year with the firm!

A focus on employee needs isn't limited to the private sector. The Department of Energy was recognized in 2000 as one of the winners of the U.S. Office of Personnel Management's awards for outstanding work/life programs. The DOE's more than 14,000 employees enjoy a wide assortment of programs, including the following:

▶ Nine child-care centers nationwide, which are fully accredited or in the process of obtaining accreditation.

▶ A "babies in the workplace" program, which involves having the child in the parent's immediate work area until the child is six months old or begins to crawl.

▶ An elder-care program consisting of comprehensive resources, counseling, and educational services.

▶ High employee participation in alternative work schedules and leave-sharing programs.

➤ Health and wellness programs that include physical fitness facilities, medical staff and industrial hygienists, brown bag seminars on a wide range of health and wellness issues, and immunizations and advisory information for employees traveling overseas.

Today, organizations are finding that they must become increasingly creative and innovative when it comes to motivating and retaining employees. They're offering a number of creative incentives, benefits, and services that are designed to make employees' lives easier and more stress free — at work and at home. For example:

Bill Payment Services

First there was direct deposit. Now more and more people are choosing to have payments for everything from daycare to utility bills taken electronically from their accounts, avoiding the need to write checks, address envelopes, or buy stamps. These are simple things, but busy professionals find these little time-consumers can add up. A growing number of on-line service providers and an expanding list of employers are offering on-line bill paying as a benefit to busy employees. Instead of getting a paper bill, their monthly bills are sent to the online service provider they've chosen. Costs vary, but are generally established on a monthly basis. Employers are often able to negotiate substantial quantity discounts on the behalf of their employees.

Catalogs and Company Stores

Options like catalogs or company stores offer a variety of products and allow employees to choose among them. These programs generally allow employees to earn points that can then be used to purchase products that they select from a catalog or store. The variety meets employees' varying needs, and employers are limited only by their imagination in coming up with criteria for awarding points.

Concierge Services

Employees — male and female — are increasingly struggling with the need to balance challenging careers with personal and family pressures. Concierge services can meet a variety of employee needs, from finding a housekeeper, to finding a unique gift for a friend, to taking care of the grocery shopping. Typically, the cost of providing the concierge service is borne by the employer, with the employee picking up the cost for any products received.

Relocation Assistance

It used to be that when a company asked an employee to move, the response was, "Where?" Not anymore. Employees are becoming increasingly reticent to relocate, particularly when it means uprooting their families. To help retain employees and to encourage relocation, employers are offering relocation assistance — not just for the employee and not just for the employee's spouse, but for the entire family. Relocation service companies provide counsel and practical assistance to employees and their families, everything from helping to find a new home, to researching the availability of soccer teams, violin lessons, riding stables — you name it.

Spiritual Counsel

Religion in the workplace? They don't call it that, but a growing number of organizations are addressing the spiritual needs of employees by offering chaplains and chaplaincy services at work. In many cases, these services are an adjunct to a corporate employee assistance program, but quite different. Chaplain services may range from the simple (someone to talk to) to the complex (arranging funeral services for an employee or an employee's family member). Companies using these services point both to a desire to address the needs of the whole employee, and to a measurable positive impact on absenteeism, turnover, and health insurance costs.

A variety of benefits to meet employee and organizational needs

As we've seen it doesn't always take grand gestures to provide meaningful benefits to employees. Here is a list of a variety of benefits commonly — and not so commonly — offered by employers. Some are simple; some are more complex. Are there items on the list that you could, or should, be offering to your employees?

> ► *Classified advertising:* Allowing employees the opportunity to run classified ads in the company newsletter or on the company intranet site can be a simple, no-cost way to provide a benefit that has a positive impact the employee's pocketbook.

> ► *Company property:* Can employees borrow the office laptop to take home for personal use? Is the company van available for employees' use during a personal move?

- *Contributions:* Employees and their families may be involved in a wide variety of programs that are very important to them. A policy/practice regarding if and when the organization will consider donations to those activities can be highly rewarding to employees. A $25 contribution to support an employee's daughter's participation in a high school athletic event may not seem like much, but it can go a long way toward establishing good will with that employee.

- *EAPs (Employee Assistance Programs):* Employee assistance programs are a way to help identify and solve concerns in the lives of employees. Family and marriage problems, stress and depression, alcohol and drug abuse, and legal, financial, career, and health issues are addressed through these plans. EAPs offer confidential help and provide time for employees to resolve issues that may be having a negative impact on their work performance.

- *Educational opportunities:* Many companies offer educational opportunities to employees to encourage them to improve the skills required to perform their current jobs as well as to help them develop skills that might be appropriate for future jobs. Both employee and company benefit.

- *Food:* Bagels in the morning. Box lunches at a noon meeting. Snacks in the afternoon. A scheduled pot luck for the department. Food can be a great motivator and it doesn't have to represent a major effort or cost.

- *Gift funds:* Birthdays. Weddings. Illnesses. Retirements. These events are milestones in employees' lives. Some organizations have funds that provide flowers or cards for employees in recognition of these events.

- *Health insurance buy back:* Health-care coverage costs have risen dramatically over the past several years and represent an important benefit to employees. But not all employees take advantage of the plan offered by their company (in two paycheck families, many employees may be covered by their spouses' insurance). Some companies offer buy-back plans, offering incentives for employees to waive health coverage through the company where they work when they are already covered under a spouse's plan.

- *Internet access:* The Internet can be a great business tool. It also has some personal applications that employees appreciate, such as on-line shopping and bill payment. Allowing staff to use the corporate Internet for personal use (as long as that use doesn't interfere with their work or involve illegal activities) can be a simple and inexpensive way to motivate staff.

- *Moonlighting:* Are employees allowed to participate in second jobs or outside professional interests as long as they do not interfere or compete with their jobs at your organization? This form of self-expression can be important to employees — to the staffer who sells gift baskets, or the employee who does freelance writing, for example.

- *Parties:* Whether an impromptu celebration to recognize a major employee effort, or a planned event (summer picnic, holiday party, etc.), parties can be a great way to recognize the efforts of employees and encourage interactions among staff in an informal setting.

- *Personal mail:* Are employees allowed to receive or send personal mail from the workplace? During the holidays, some companies allow their mailrooms to package and mail materials for staff (staff pays the cost of postage). Some companies, on the other hand, don't allow employees to drop personal mail (even postage-paid personal mail) into the company's mail system.

- *Profit sharing:* Profit-sharing plans can be a good way to tie employee performance to company results, with benefits to employees directly tied to those results. Plans and plan elements will vary by company.

- *Smoking:* The issue of smoking on company premises has become fraught with controversy. While non-smokers resent the impact that secondhand smoke may have upon their health, smokers feel their rights are being threatened when smoking prohibitions are too restrictive. A possible solution might be the establishment of a separately vented area where smokers can partake without impacting their fellow employees.

- *Smoking cessation:* In the interest of helping employees who wish to quit smoking, some companies subsidize or pay for smoking cessation programs. Others may offer rewards to employees who are able to go without cigarettes for certain pre-designated periods of time.

► *Tuition reimbursement:* Tuition reimbursement programs provide payment for a portion, or all, of the costs of employees pursuing advanced degrees in programs related to their current or potential jobs within a company.

Communicating the value of employee benefits

Do your employees really appreciate the value of the benefits they receive as part of their employment package? The answer may very well be "No," and the reason may very well be that your company doesn't do enough to communicate to employees the value of the benefits they receive.

Studies have shown that companies may spend as much as 42 percent of their payroll on fringe benefits. An employee earning $30,000 a year, then, would be receiving additional benefits worth $12,600. But that employee is unlikely to realize the value of those benefits.

Communication is the key to ensuring that employees know about the value of the benefits they receive. This can be done during recruitment and orientation. It can also be done on a regular basis by including information about benefits in employee publications, encouraging managers to remind employees of the value of their benefits at review time and when salary issues are discussed, and by including benefit information prominently in employee handbooks or on company intranets.

Personalized benefit statements are another good way to ensure that employees realize the value of the benefits you're providing.

Corporations are becoming increasingly creative and noticeably less conservative in coming up with benefits and services to attract and retain employees. But in spite of the number of creative options available to aid employee retention, companies can't afford to forget the basics. Employees want to be recognized for the contributions they make.

8

RECOGNITION AND REWARD

The manager of a marketing department was concerned that her employees weren't being aggressive or proactive enough in using new technologies to do their jobs. Trying to push them through weekly meetings wasn't working. Bringing in examples of what their local colleagues were doing wasn't working. Offering the opportunity for them to attend training programs on new technology wasn't working. Including work-plan items in their annual reviews wasn't working. Finally, after a conversation with her manager, she introduced a recognition and reward program designed to encourage innovation. Called the Innovation Award, the program offered a $100 gift certificate for the most innovative application of technology introduced during the previous quarter.

The award was offered four times each year and the work group itself voted on each application. Employees were encouraged to work in partners to present ideas, and work together to come up with unique and innovative ways of applying technology. Each applicant or group of applicants prepared a written summary of the idea, how technology was applied, and how the idea would save time, money, or improve service. Each entry would then be described in detail at a staff meeting, and other work-group members would have the ability to ask questions and rate each entry.

The result? A higher level of awareness of how technology — even simple applications of technology, such as using the laser printer to label mailings instead of printing labels and applying them by hand — could be used to improve the performance of the department. Healthy competition was created among the staff to see who could come up with the most creative application of technology, which was particularly challenging for those employees whose jobs didn't obviously use technology applications. But the most important result was recognition.

Companies have historically used a wide variety of mechanisms to recognize and reward employees. Much of the process of motivating employees involves the day-to-day business of setting goals, providing feedback, involving employees in decisions, and recognizing their efforts. These techniques are becoming the norm. Beyond these standard practices, however, lies of wealth of strategies that creative companies are using.

At CyberSource in Mountain View, California, the employee of the month gets a BMW Z3 to drive and park in front of the building. "Carpe Cash" is also available to employees who want to recognize their coworkers. Employees can give these vouchers to others whom they feel are going above and beyond the call of duty. Carpe Cash is redeemable for lunch in the company cafeteria or at local establishments, as well as for company logo items.

At JM Family Enterprises, Inc., an automotive company in Deerfield Beach, Florida, a number of programs are offered for associates. These include award programs, Work/Life resources, referral and concierge programs, an on-site medical center with physicians and nurses, free haircuts and manicures, dry cleaning services, 30 paid days off per year, fitness centers, an indoor lap-swimming pool (open 24 hours), use of company plans for emergencies (when available), and more. The firm was named as one of the "Best Companies to Work For" in *Fortune magazine*'s 2000 poll.

JM recognizes associates who exemplify the company's "three Cs: consideration, cooperation, and communication," and who "embody the spirit and true culture of the company."

At Fenwick & West, a law firm and another of *Fortune Magazine*'s "Best Companies to Work For," employees are recognized annually through a staff appreciation day. At the most recent event, employees were provided with a certificate offering a number of choices:

- A crisp $100 bill (the firm paid the taxes)
- A Sony DVD player
- A one-year family pass to Marriott's Great America
- A one-year family pass to Santa Cruz Beach Boardwalk
- Two days off work with full pay

In addition to Staff Appreciation Day, Fenwick & West holds an annual "Best of Fenwick" awards ceremony, in which employees who are selected by their peers as stellar performers are honored in a number of categories, including —

- outstanding role model for corporate citizenship,
- outstanding effort in communication,
- making the workplace fun,
- outstanding mentoring and training,
- outstanding leadership in a crisis,
- rookie of the year,
- special award for charitable work, and
- firm culture award.

The firm wisely recognizes that employees come in all shapes and sizes, represent different ages, and have different interests and priorities. When it comes to reward and recognition, one size most certainly does not fit all!

At STC Associations, a communications agency and consultancy in New York City, employees are offered "sumptuous vacations" as part of a resort-club membership called Private Retreats. "We chose the Private Retreats concept because our employees have a unique need for rest and relaxation," says STC CEO Sophie Ann Terrisse. "They easily burn out in the demanding, creative industry in which we work."

At the AIM Companies, an international group that provides nutritional education and natural products, the AIM Bucks program allows employees to nominate their peers for reward. The nomination form is sent over the company intranet to the employees' supervisor, who decides how many AIM Bucks the nomination is worth and gives the employees the reward. AIM Bucks can be used to purchase a variety of items on the "AIM Bucks Inventory List," including one paid day off, various gift certificates, or passes to local recreational sites and movie theatres.

"I think the majority of companies do have formal recognition programs in place," says Greg Boswell, a National Association of Employee Recognition board member, and manager of market research with the O.C. Tanner Company in Salt Lake City. "I know that well over 80 percent of the Fortune 500 have, at a minimum, service award programs."

Debra Sikanas, president of Baudville, a Grand Rapids firm that markets award and recognition solutions, agrees. "Although I don't have a way to measure how prevalent these programs are," she says, "I can speak as a resource provider. We're seeing tremendous growth in both formal and informal programs. Our customers come in all shapes and sizes, as do their needs and budgets." Companies, she says, "are seeking the next level, having experienced or read about the benefits of recognition."

The simple things

While many companies make grand gestures when it comes to reward and recognition, even the smallest companies with the most limited budgets can provide motivating rewards.

More than money, employees often cite the intangible or "soft" aspects of corporate culture as having a strong influence on their commitment. These include low-cost or no-cost aspects, such as attentive, people-oriented management, or an employee's confidence that the organization would help in a time of need.

Think about it. If you start from the premise that the vast majority of employees truly want to do a good job, doesn't it make sense that they also want to hear about it when they've performed effectively?

Simple recognition can be extremely motivating. Recognition doesn't cost anything, and it takes very little time to say, "You did a great job with that report. The background research and data you presented was very convincing. Thanks for your help."

Recognition is a very effective and accessible way to motivate your employees. It is also a tool that you have at your immediate disposal.

Here are some tips:

► Make yourself available to talk to your people. Your simply being there is very important to the people who work for you. If you say you have an open-door policy, abide by it. Your undivided and sincere attention to your employees is extremely motivating.

► Encourage people to work with you, not for you. Teamwork is more than a buzzword: it is an important way to encourage employees to meet department and company objectives. To reword a familiar saying, When your employees feel they are a part of the solution, they won't be a part of the problem.

► Tell your employees in advance about changes that affect them. As we'll see in the next chapter, involvement is another essential key to motivation.

► Give credit when due. Be quick to compliment.

► Make sure each person knows what is expected and how he or she is doing.

Employees need to know what behaviors will be rewarded and what behaviors will be criticized. Make your expectations clear. Be sure your employees understand what these expectations are and how they fit into the overall goals of the company.

Simple guidelines? Certainly. Recognition is simple. But, perhaps because it's so simple, it's often overlooked. Don't fall into the trap that keeps many supervisors from developing a motivated staff. Be sure that you:

► Recognize employee motivators and dismotivators. Again, remember that each employee is different. Get to know each of your employees and what motivates them. One manager tells of a time when she almost made a fatal error in recognizing a staff member. A graphic designer had come up with a great idea for providing a "wall of fame" in the organization's breakroom to recognize staff members who went above and beyond the call of duty. The manager thought it would be a great idea to recognize the graphic designer publicly at the next staff meeting. Fortunately, she forgot herself, and mentioned to the designer her plan. The designer was appalled. She hated public recognition and would have been extremely uncomfortable being put on display. The lesson? Don't assume you know the type of recognition that will motivate your employees.

- ▶ Help employees set clear goals. Employees can't be rewarded if they're not performing up to department or company standards. And they can't perform if they don't know what those standards are. As a supervisor or manager, you need to work with each employee to set clear goals and to make sure that your employees know, specifically, what they need to do to meet those goals. Then, when they meet them, you need to recognize their efforts.

- ▶ Provide motivational performance reviews. Performance reviews are not only meant to correct behavior or put through a request for a salary increase. These can be great opportunities for managers to motivate employees. There are two parts to any performance review: a discussion of past performance, including recognition of goal attainment or instances in which the employee has exceeded expectations, and a look at the goals and challenges for the coming year. This is an opportunity to focus on what the employee does right, building on those positive skills to establish goals for the next time period.

- ▶ Give credit and praise for accomplishments. Don't overlook the little things that your employees do on a regular basis. It is unfortunate that sometimes the best performers are virtually ignored, while their less capable coworkers receive the bulk of the manager's attention. Too many managers take the approach that no news is good news, and don't take the time to recognize the positive, everyday efforts of their staff.

- ▶ Develop effective reward systems. Coming up with ways to recognize and reward employees can be challenging — and fun. Be creative. A humorous traveling trophy can have as much impact on performance as a cash award. Involve your employees in the process of developing rewards as well as recognizing their peers. They often notice things that you don't!

Problems with awards

Why do some employers and managers fail to establish formal reward and recognition programs for their employees? In many cases, it is due to concerns of fairness and consistency. Providing employees with awards does present some problems. A common concern is that rewarding employees in even a small way can lead to competition and jealousy. Letting this concern keep you from offering awards to outstanding employees is unnecessary, however. To deal with possible jealousies, companies have tried the following:

▶ Giving individual awards to all members of a project team so that no individual feels slighted

▶ Structuring the award system so that awards go only to those whose achievements are outstanding and widely recognized

In addition to competition and jealousy, there is another concern: the decision to grant or withhold an award is an employment decision. As such, it is subject to all the laws, regulations, and guidelines that apply to any other type of employment decision. Consequently, with any type of program you establish, it is important that you —

▶ require a review of awards by the employee-relations staff or other impartial party,

▶ keep the criteria for awards broad, and

▶ make sure your administrative procedures are fair and well monitored.

The type of award program that will be most helpful to the company, whether different levels of awards should be included, and who should be eligible to participate needs to be decided before a successful program can be established. Naturally, determining what type of program will best suit the interests of the company depends upon what behaviors and activities the company wishes to reward.

How can you establish a good system for rewarding your employees? Following are some simple guidelines:

▶ Tie incentives to results. Make it quite obvious to employees what they need to do to be rewarded.

▶ Consider the needs and abilities of the entire staff, not just your top performers. Consider providing rewards to novices for their efforts to learn rather than their ability to produce.

▶ Ask for input and advice from your employees when determining rewards and guidelines for winners. Your employees will often set higher standards for themselves than you do, and will appreciate the fact that you asked for their input.

▶ Make sure that top management is committed to the program.

▶ Make the program flexible and adapt it to special situations.

- Provide rewards that are consistent with the performance goals you set.

- Let your employees know what's in it for them.

- Avoid the temptation to reward poor performers by making exceptions.

Rewarding employee longevity

In an era of organizations being as concerned about maintaining competitive advantage as retaining employees, the issue of whether (and how) to reward employee longevity can be a vexing one. Should employees be rewarded for years of service, or should rewards be based on competence and contribution? If not monetary awards, what about recognition? After all, with unemployment levels at their lowest in years, and the one-company career virtually a thing of the past, it can be tough to keep good employees.

There are no easy answers and no clear-cut guidelines. Solutions vary and appropriately reflect the unique culture and business climate of each organization.

Should longevity be rewarded? Many say no. But longevity should be recognized. When employees are rewarded for length of service as opposed to contributions to the organization, there can be a tendency for complacency to set in. This can have a demoralizing affect on shorter-term staff members, who are often enthusiastic, creative, and willing to suggest new ideas that longer-term staff members may be less likely to identify, or more likely to respond to with comments such as, "We tried that before and it didn't work."

The bottom line is that longevity doesn't necessarily correspond to productivity or efficacy. As one manager points out, "Paying someone because they've been around a long time can be a real disincentive to someone with less years of service and twice as much drive and ability."

The solution? Look for ways to recognize longevity that don't impact compensation. Consider the following examples:

- An annual appreciation night to recognize employees reaching various levels of service.

- Service awards.

➤ Simple gifts. Work with a local jeweler to design a pin based on your company logo that can be provided to employees who reach a certain longevity milestone.

➤ Contract with a vendor that offers a catalog of gifts from which employees may choose; selection from various categories may depend upon the employee's years of service.

➤ Recognize employees on their anniversaries in the company newsletter, at staff meetings, or on the corporate intranet.

➤ Take employees to lunch on their anniversaries.

Service recognition shouldn't stop with employees. If your company works with volunteers or board members, these individuals deserve recognition as well. Even CEOs need to be recognized!

When it comes to rewarding and recognizing longevity, says Lynda Ford, balance is key. Ford is president of The Ford Group, an HR consulting firm in Lee Center, N.Y. "Longevity along does not a great employee make," says Ford, "so while you want to have something that recognizes the fact that they have spent time with you, you also want to place more emphasis on their performance, their contributions, and the value they bring to the organization."

Ford also warns against waiting for the magical five-year point to recognize an employee's contributions. "Let's face it," she says, "you're not going to get a chance to recognize half of your workforce if you wait that long!

"Today, it's not unusual to look at somebody's résumé and see three jobs in the last five years. We're living in a time where everything happens quickly and people want more instant gratification. We need to rethink how we reward for seniority."

One way of doing this, she says, is by taking into account the individuality of each employee. "Not everybody wants a certificate. Not everyone wants a pin. There are different ways of recognizing people."

But successful recognition goes beyond selection of the right award. Successful recognition should be ongoing — and should not occur too late.

People entering the workforce today have a much different perspective than did their parents. While recognition of employee contributions through their years of service is certainly an important element of any company's retention efforts, it's only part of the picture. Take a critical look at all the mechanisms in place for recognizing and rewarding employees — from the simple, verbal praise that we are all capable of, to the more complex and more expensive rewards, such as vacation packages. Regardless of industry, regardless of size, regardless of financial standing, any company can come up with creative and effective ways to recognize the efforts of its employees.

Additional resources

The National Association for Employee Recognition (www .recognition.org) is dedicated to the enhancement of employee performance through recognition, including its strategies and related initiatives. The association provides a forum for information and best-practices sharing, as well as education to foster the use, excitement, effectiveness, and enthusiasm of recognition.

(1801 N. Mill St., Suite R, Naperville, IL 60563; 1-630-369-7783; <NAER@recognition.org>.)

WorldatWork (www.worldatwork.org), formerly the American Compensation Association and Canadian Compensation Association, is a 45-year-old global not-for-profit professional association dedicated to knowledge leadership in disciplines associated with attracting, retaining, and motivating employees. WorldatWork emphasizes total rewards, specifically focusing on compensation and benefits, as well as other components of the work experience such as work/life balance, recognition, culture, professional development, and work environment. In addition, WorldatWork offers certification and education programs, online information resources, publications, conferences, research, and networking opportunities.

(WorldatWork US and International office: 14040 N. Northsight Blvd.,Scottsdale, AZ 85260; 877-951-9191; <customerrelations @worldatwork.org>. WorldatWork Canadian office: P.O. Box 9455, Postal Station A, Toronto, Ontario, M5W 4E1; 877-951-9191; <worldatwork@associationsfirst.com>.)

9

INVOLVEMENT AND ADVANCEMENT

Will employees exceed expectations even if they're not offered additional pay to do so? Can work itself be motivating? Yes, it can.

"One of the most motivating things to me," says a manager at an energy company, "is being asked to take on a new project." But, she adds, "it's only motivating if the assignment comes from somebody I respect — a mentor. And the assignment needs to have a positive impact on the organization. I need to know that I will make a difference."

Making a difference matters. The 1999 Employee Relationship Report Benchmark conducted by Walker Information and Hudson Institute reflects the attitudes and experiences of workers in business, government, and nonprofit organizations. The survey generated 2293 responses — a remarkable 75 percent return from a mailing of 3075. Three-quarters of the employees said they will often do things at work that are "above and beyond the call of duty," and roughly the same number feel highly motivated to do their job well.

Walker segmented respondents into four groups based on their predicted loyalty to their employer. The breakdown is as follows:

1) Truly loyal employees (24 percent) feel an attachment to their organization — they want to be there and they intend to stay

for at least two years. These employees feel good about the organization and their place in it. Typically high performers, they are willing to go the extra mile to get the job done and often act as role models for their peers.

2) Accessible employees (4 percent) are similar to the Truly Loyal, but do not intend to stay with their employers, sometimes because of perceptions of limited career advancement opportunities, sometimes because of external factors (a spouse's relocation, for instance). However, in spite of their limited tenure, these employees generally perform well and will put forth extra effort during their employment.

3) Trapped employees (39 percent) are less loyal to the organization and unlikely to want to stay, yet they feel they must stay — they are, in essence, trapped. They are typically poorer performers who are not likely to excel in their positions.

4) High-risk employees (33 percent) are also low commitment. Not only do they not want to be with the organization, they also don't intend to stay.

The study also found that commitment varied by industry, company size, and position. Employees in the Utility and Public Administration/Government sectors are more likely to stay with their companies (76 percent and 71 percent) than employees in Business Services (51 percent), Retail Trade (56 percent), and Technology (56 percent).

Small companies and entrepreneurs, defined as having 99 or fewer workers, performed better than the larger organizations on many loyalty measures, particularly on feeling part of the organization, having a strong personal attachment to the organization, and believing that the organization deserves their loyalty. Employees in these small companies also exhibit a stronger feeling of obligation to stay, and rate their at-work factors more positively than employees of larger companies.

Commitment to the workplace was lower at lower levels in the organization. Upper-management employees were more likely to feel part of a team and have strong personal attachments to the organization.

You want your employees to fall into the "truly loyal" or "accessible" categories — you want to avoid having "trapped" or "high-risk" employees. Today's employers and managers need to find ways of engaging employees so that they feel a part of the workplace and will be committed and loyal to the company. It's not enough to engender that level of commitment in only the upper echelons of the organization — all employees must be engaged, from the receptionist to the facilities engineer, to the secretary, the salesperson, the production-line worker, and the accountant.

How can employees become engaged? By being provided with opportunities to participate in decision-making and by seeing ways in which they can advance in the company, increasing the impact that they, individually, have on the organization.

Focus groups, project teams, advisory boards — these are just a few of the many ways in which companies can involve employees in the activities of their organizations. Why does it makes sense to involve employees in decisions? Practically speaking, because they represent a wealth of knowledge about how the organization really works. They are on the front lines, so to speak, and the information and experiences they have can be extremely informative.

Employees may be involved in decisions as basic as whether to charge employees for coffee or as far-reaching as whether to start an employee stock-ownership plan.

It is important to note that employee involvement is meant here to indicate opportunities for employees to be included in decisions about their work and about the organization's initiatives. It is not intended to refer to any aspects of collective bargaining that would take place in a unionized environment. In collective bargaining, the employees negotiate with management through the union, which speaks for the employees as an exclusive voice. The discussions here refer only to involvement as it occurs in non-union environments.

Employee involvement allows a company to share decision making. Employees then become directly responsible for the work they do.

Today's corporate leaders know the importance of employee involvement and how it can affect profits. Employees can be a company's most valuable resource. As more companies come to realize just how valuable their employees really are, they are making efforts to increase involvement.

The changing workforce also contributes to the need for employee involvement. Putting it simply, employees are demanding to be involved.

Employee involvement was first used to keep employees happy. As workers became more demanding, management felt a strong push to provide better working conditions, better benefits, and more involvement in the decision-making process.

What a surprise to discover that once these employees became involved, strange things began to happen. Motivation increased. Productivity increased. There were more new ideas. Innovative techniques, processes, and products were introduced. And, ultimately, the bottom line was fattened. Something that was started to keep employees satisfied led to a direct, positive impact on company profits.

Decision making: More than a managerial prerogative

The change in managerial attitude has, perhaps, paralleled the change in parental attitude. Today's parents are allowing their children a more equal role in family decisions; today's corporations are allowing employees a more equal role in corporate decisions.

Managers are realizing, and rightly so, that employees are more likely to participate in an activity to which they are committed. They are more likely to be committed if they are involved in the decision-making process behind the development of the activity.

There are two very important reasons why managers should strive for employee participation in decision making:

1) Reduced resentment over taking orders. As we've already implied, employees don't like being pushed around. If employees are given orders and allowed no input, you will see lowered morale, poor attitude, and increased turnover.

2) Employees know more than you do! When it comes to the day-to-day operation of your company or department, nobody knows what will work better than the job holder. Nobody can offer better information on changes to procedures, policies, or operations than the person who does the job, day after day, week after week, and month after month. If you don't gather input from these people, you are likely to be hurting yourself and your company.

Consider the following example:

Jackie was the personnel director of a small consulting company. As the company grew, departments developed and employees were divided by specialty (i.e., planning, promotion, production). The clerical staff, however, remained a separate group, bull-pen style. Jackie found that evaluating these employees was becoming very difficult. Each clerical person worked with one or two middle-management people. However, daily work assignments were given by a service coordinator who was also responsible for semi-annual reviews. Jackie felt that this did not allow for valuable input from the middle-management people.

Jackie, with permission from upper management, decided to assign clerical people to specific departments. This is what happened:

➤ *Because clerical workers were now located throughout the company, they felt isolated from each other.*

➤ *More clerical workers were hired in some departments. In other departments, clerical workers often had nothing to do. There was no longer a central service coordinator to monitor and distribute assignments.*

➤ *Morale suffered. In individual departments, clerical workers began to feel as though they were at the bottom of the totem pole.*

What went wrong here? Certainly Jackie's idea was not out of line with the experiences of other companies. In fact, many companies have clerical staff assigned to specific departments and don't experience the problems that Jackie encountered.

Putting it quite simply, Jackie failed to involve the people who should have been involved in making the decision — namely, the job holders. While she consulted with management, she didn't seek input from the clerical workers or from their service coordinator.

If she had, she would have learned about possible problems. The biggest error is not involving the involved.

Is it necessary to involve employees in all decisions? It is if the individuals will be affected by the decision. We all accept orders more easily if we've offered our own opinions and suggestions before a decision is made. You may not use every comment or suggestion an employee makes. However, by involving your employees, you will have more information to support your decisions. You'll increase your chance of making a decision that has a positive effect on motivation and productivity.

Encouraging employee involvement

Before employees can become involved, they need information and education. They need to understand what the company's goals are and how their activities help to meet those goals. They need to learn the skills necessary to be part of a fully functioning team.

It's not enough to simply tell employees: "We want you to be more involved." The foundation for that involvement needs to be clearly defined and developed.

First, make sure that upper management is committed to the concept of employee involvement. Involvement starts at the top. If there is managerial resistance, there will be a breakdown in the organization.

Provide orientation training seminars to present your philosophy on involvement and to secure enthusiastic commitment. Start with upper management and then help management introduce the concepts to others, one level at a time.

Make sure that top management objectives are presented to all levels of the company so goals can be established.

Evaluate performance based on the accomplishment of these goals.

Develop a system of weekly meetings involving all employees. At these meetings, discuss any problems that may have developed, provide clarification, or revise objectives that are unsatisfactory in any way.

Encourage employees to express their opinions at any time. Make special efforts to keep communication channels open.

There are many benefits that can be realized through increased involvement of employees in the activities of your company. These include —

- ▶ increased motivation of employees and managers;
- ▶ more time for managers to manage, due to the group effort put toward meeting goals;
- ▶ clear-cut goals, making it easier for managers and employees to devote their time to activities that have the greatest pay-off for the company;
- ▶ improved coordination and teamwork among all personnel;

- more equitable salary distribution, with compensation based on results;

- improved communication, with the entire company working toward mutual goals; and

- easier performance evaluation, since performance is judged on specific accomplishments rather than subjective or generalized opinions.

"What do you think?"

How many times have you or other managers in your company wondered what your employees think? The best way to discover what your employees think is to ask them. While face-to-face discussions are always best, in large companies, asking each employee individually for his or her opinion on a particular subject can be time consuming and inefficient. In these cases, or when you're looking for a more objective measure of employee opinion, attitude surveys can be the answer.

Attitude surveys can measure employees' feelings on their jobs, their supervisors, their coworkers, company benefits, overall management, and the quality of products and services produced. There are two important things you must consider before doing an employee attitude survey. You and the company must be prepared to —

1) report the results of the survey to employees, and

2) take action based on the results of the surveys.

If you are unwilling to follow either of these two guidelines, there is no point in conducting an attitude survey.

Company morale will be improved by listening to and acting on employee suggestions. If you are going to the trouble of conducting an employee attitude survey, you must be prepared to act on the comments and suggestions you receive. Attitude surveys are valuable for monitoring the feelings of employees. Whether you design a survey specifically for your company or use a standardized survey, the information you receive will provide you with the following:

- A measure of employee perception of the organization's strengths and weaknesses

- A measure of how effective management is at managing

- An opportunity for encouraging employee communication of thoughts, feelings, concerns, suggestions, and complaints
- A yardstick against which to compare previous and future survey results to determine whether the company is improving

A company can't successfully plan or implement change without input from its employees. Attitude surveys can provide you with the information you need.

Encouraging employee suggestions

Nine out of ten employees responding to a survey by IABC/William Mercer said they felt they had good ideas to offer their companies, but more than half of them said there was a lack of management interest in their ideas — 25 percent feeling that management "doesn't care" about their ideas and another 25 percent indicating that their companies didn't offer a good time or a good way for them to share ideas.

While many companies have some form of employee suggestion program in place, too often these programs are ineffective. Following are some keys for ensuring that your company has the right environment for encouraging employees to share ideas and suggestions:

- Ensure that managers are open to employee ideas. In some cases, managers may feel threatened by employee suggestions and may react defensively. "We've already tried that and it didn't work!" is a common response to ideas that employees share. Certainly this can be a valid reply. But encouraging managers to be open to ideas and to consider even the ideas that aren't necessarily new can go a long way toward building an environment in which employees feel comfortable bringing forth their thoughts and opinions. Change occurs rapidly in today's business environment. An idea that wasn't appropriate a year ago — or even a few months ago — may be very appropriate today.

- Involve managers in the process. Rather than encouraging employees to bypass their managers when submitting ideas, encourage employees to use their managers as the first point of contact when submitting ideas.

- Guide employee input. Managers sometimes become frustrated by the tone or content of employee suggestions. "Put more diet soda in the soda machine," "Make our breaks longer," and "Give us more time off" are self-serving suggestions that are not directed at meeting company needs. Make it clear to employees what type of ideas you're looking for. Establish reward systems to recognize those ideas that fit the criteria, thereby sending a signal to employees about what type of ideas are valued.

► Keep it simple. Complicated suggestion programs won't be used by employees who simply want a quick and easy way to share their thoughts and ideas. Technology can simplify this process. If you have a corporate intranet, an on-line forum can be used to generate and share ideas. E-mail is another possibility.

► Show support of even those ideas that aren't implemented. Some employees will be hesitant to share ideas for fear of being criticized or ridiculed. Responses such as, "We're already doing that!" or, "That will never work!" will quickly make employees non-communicative. Even ideas that can't be implemented should be valued. Communicating with employees whose ideas are rejected is even more critical than communicating with those whose ideas are implemented. Make sure you thank the employee for the idea and clearly explain why it can't or won't be implemented. Rejected ideas present a great opportunity for you to educate employees about the types of ideas you are looking for.

► Allow anonymous input. Managers often feel that employees should be required to sign their names to their suggestions. Some employees are comfortable with that. Many may not be. A lot depends on the culture of your organization. But remember that while managers may feel comfortable taking a risk with sharing an idea that may or may not be implemented, many employees feel hesitant to do so — particularly if their suggestion contains an element of criticism or may reflect negatively on their manager or workgroup. The less an employee has to risk in submitting an idea, the more likely that employee will be to share his or her input.

► Be responsive. Ideas that languish in somebody's in-box for weeks or months send a very direct and negative message to employees: "We don't care." Immediate follow-up is important and may be as simple as saying, "We've received your suggestion and it is currently being evaluated." Beyond this immediate acknowledgement, make sure you do evaluate the idea as quickly as possible and respond directly to the employee about the resolution of his or her idea.

- ➤ Use ideas as an opportunity for recognition. Seek ways of communicating ideas and their resolution to all staff members — perhaps in your employee publication or on the company intranet. This does two things: 1) it lets all staff know the type of ideas that are valued, and 2) it provides recognition for those employees who are submitting valuable suggestions.

Job growth and opportunity

Not everyone likes everything about his or her job. In fact, some people don't like anything about the jobs they do. You probably know some of these people. You probably have some of them working in your organization, perhaps even working for you.

What do you do with people who don't seem to like what they do? How should you handle people who don't perform to capacity, who come in late, call in sick, and are slow in production?

If you're truly interested in providing a motivating environment for all your employees, your answer won't be "Fire them," because terminations are unmotivating not only for the person being terminated, but also for the workers who keep their jobs. In many cases, it isn't the employee that's the problem anyway — it's the job itself.

Psychologist Frederick Herzberg said, "The proper attitude for a man in a Mickey Mouse job is a Mickey Mouse attitude." Many theorists agree with him, at least in principle.

Employees want jobs that are challenging. They want to be able to take pride in their accomplishments. They are interested in autonomy and variety.

What makes a job a good job?

A good job will provide —

- ➤ *Natural units of work:* Employees will be able to see a beginning and an end to their tasks.

- ➤ *Meaningful goals:* Clear and moderately difficult goals give employees something to shoot for. Participation in goal setting encourages commitment instead of compliance. Goals should be set high enough to be challenging. Goals shouldn't be so high, however, that they are impossible to reach.

► *Direct feedback:* A goal is meaningful only if employees can get quick, direct information on how they're doing. It's best if this feedback can come from the work itself.

► *Client relationships:* Employees should have direct contact with the users of their products or services. These users may be inside or outside the company.

► *Autonomy:* Jobs should be designed in such a way that job holders are involved in setting their schedules, choosing work methods, troubleshooting, checking on quality, training other workers, and problem-solving.

Incorporating these points into your management structure will enable the company to meet the job holder's needs for achievement, recognition, satisfaction, responsibility, growth, and advancement.

Keep in mind, however, that not all employees are looking for more responsibility or more work. Some employees may view attempts to improve their jobs as simply giving them more than they can handle. Forcing someone to take on more responsibility can result in negative effects.

Providing job growth

What are some of the techniques you can use to provide job growth to those employees who seek additional challenge? Consider such options as —

► job redesign,

► job enlargement,

► job restructuring,

► job enrichment,

► cross-training, and

► teambuilding.

Let's look at each of these options in more detail.

Job redesign

Many jobs are poorly designed. They do not help productivity or encourage employee enthusiasm. The problem lies in job design. Formerly, job design was based on five general rules:

- ➤ Skills should be specialized
- ➤ Skill requirements should be minimized
- ➤ Training time should be minimized
- ➤ The number and variety of tasks in a job should be limited
- ➤ The job should be as repetitive as possible

This approach to job design created positions that were, in effect, too easy. Dividing work into parts that are too small leads to over-specialization, which in turn can cause fatigue, apathy, absenteeism, grievances, reduced productivity, work stoppages, and high turnover. Specialization uses only a portion of worker abilities. The result is bored, unenthusiastic workers who eventually lose all motivation.

Jobs need to be designed so that workers —

- ➤ are given responsibilities and challenges that match their skills, abilities, and expectations;
- ➤ have a sense of wholeness in their work;
- ➤ can more easily identify their contributions to the organization's objectives;
- ➤ can participate in decisions that affect their jobs; and
- ➤ can control larger portions of their own work.

Job redesign involves redefining a job. Employees are given greater responsibility, allowed more control, and provided with frequent feedback. There are two broad aspects to job redesign: job enlargement and job restructuring.

Job enlargement

Job enlargement increases the number of tasks assigned to an employee. The employee's autonomy, decision-making authority, and skill level are not increased.

Job enlargement broadens the job rather than deepening the employee's responsibility. By increasing the variety of tasks, an employee is called upon to use a greater variety of knowledge and skill and is allowed more freedom and responsibility. This is often called horizontal job enrichment. For example, instead of ten workers each doing one step in a process, each worker might perform all steps and inspect the completed job.

Companies considering job enlargement programs are usually trying to reduce boredom while improving the quality of the products produced. Job enlargement makes work more interesting and challenging and aids in cost reduction.

Job restructuring

Job restructuring is an attempt to increase the depth of a job by requiring higher knowledge and skill. This is sometimes called vertical job enrichment. It gives employees added opportunity for planning and controlling their work.

The idea is that employees can manage themselves quite well if allowed to. Jobs are expanded to allow workers to participate in managerial functions like planning and controlling. Employees use their own judgment and discretion to make decisions about their work. They participate with their supervisors in problem solving and goal setting. They offer ideas, suggestions, and opinions. The employee is given greater autonomy and increased responsibility for planning, directing, and controlling the work done.

Job enrichment

Job enrichment is an important way to mesh today's business needs with the needs of employees. Businesses need able and loyal workers. Workers need to meet their higher-order needs. Job enrichment works for both of them.

J. Richard Hackman, author of *Groups That Work (and Those That Don't): Creating Conditions for Effective Teamwork* (Jossey-Bass Publishers, 1990) has identified five core characteristics of jobs that will motivate people to be high performers: skill variety, task identity (that is, the degree to which the job involves the completion of a whole and identifiable task), task significance, autonomy, and feedback. He has also identified five parallel strategies for changing the job to make it more meaningful. These strategies and the questions to ask when trying to implement them are outlined below.

▶ Form natural work units to promote the employee's sense of ownership. Ask yourself:

    i. Does the job correspond to a natural unit of work, one in which the employee can develop a sense of continuing responsibility?

    ii. Is there any basis for identifying the job with the person or department for whom it is performed?

    iii. Is work assigned randomly (without a clear focus) or naturally (in ways that promote task identity)?

▶ Combine separate tasks wherever possible. Ask yourself:

    i. Can separate tasks be combined into larger work units?

    ii. Can tasks such as setup, inspection, verification, or checking be added to existing work units?

    iii. Can responsibility for a new, larger task be assigned to a small team of workers?

▶ Establish client relationships to expand the three core dimensions of feedback, skill variety, and autonomy. Ask yourself:

    i. Do we know who is the client for the worker's services?

    ii. Can we establish direct contact between the worker and the client?

    iii. Can we set up criteria so the client can judge the quality of the product or service?

    iv. Can we give the client a way of communicating evaluations directly to employees?

▶ Give rank-and-file employees management-type responsibilities. Ask yourself:

    i. Can we give workers more responsibility for setting schedules, deciding on work methods, and helping to train less experienced employees?

    ii. Can we give workers more control over their time — when to stop and start work, take breaks, etc.?

iii. Can we encourage workers to come up with solutions to problems on their own rather than relying on their bosses for the answers?

iv. Can we provide the workers with more information about the financial aspects of their jobs?

► Feedback channels so workers can learn about performance while doing the job. Ask yourself:

i. Can we place quality control close to the workers so they get frequent feedback on performance?

ii. Can we provide workers directly with standard summaries of performance records?

iii. Can workers receive individual performance information via computer instead of secondhand?

iv. Can workers correct their own mistakes?

Supervisors and managers should always be alert for such trouble signs as high turnover, restricted output, poor quality, and excessive absenteeism. Keep the following points in mind:

► Tasks that challenge without overwhelming or underestimating the person will tend to be more motivating. Don't push too hard on employees. Make sure that when you ask an employee to do more, or to attack a new project or challenge that you also provide the employee with the tools and resources he or she will need to be successful. "Stretch goals" can be motivating, but you don't want them to become overwhelming.

► The chances for employees to become involved in their work are greater if control of the work (power to act, responsibility, and authority) is moved downward to the employees rather than upward to the boss. As a manager, you should focus on results and outcomes — not necessarily process. Employees will appreciate the opportunity to design their own systems and strategies for accomplishing goals, rather than being required to "do it your way."

► Feedback from an aspect of the work itself is a far better reinforcer of good performance than is feedback through a superior. How will employees know if they're successful? Is it possible to receive feedback based on the task or process rather than from management? For example, sales personnel have immediate feedback based on their success in selling the company's product. What aspects of the work your employees do can provide signals about success?

➤ Employees are more likely to accept added responsibility if appropriate feedback and control are included. Employees don't just want "more work." They want more meaningful work and the ability to learn and grow on the job. But feedback is important too. Employees need to be recognized and rewarded for their efforts.

➤ Don't limit opportunities to a select few. Quieter, less visible employees, can often be overlooked when opportunities present themselves and both the organization and the employee will miss out. Don't give all the plum assignments or opportunities to the "stars" on your team. You may be surprised to find that some of your less visible employees have skills, ambitions, and expertise that can contribute dramatically to your work team.

Cross-training

Cross-training provides employees with experiences in different jobs on a regular basis, and benefits management by providing more depth of experience within the workgroup. This is a vital strategy in the event of employee absence or turnover. Cross-training can occur within or between departments. Employees are given the opportunity to switch from one job to another, offering variety and helping to prevent complacency. In addition, employees learn new skills and aspects of the organization that can lead to greater job satisfaction and feelings of self-worth.

Teambuilding

Teambuilding efforts bring employees together to work as a single group. There are different types of teams that can be formed:

➤ *Operating teams:* groups of employees who perform their day-to-day tasks as a team

➤ *Problem-oriented teams and task forces:* groups of employees who come together on a temporary or permanent basis to discuss and recommend solutions to specific problems

> *Management teams:* groups of supervisory and management personnel who regularly work together to deal with operational problems, daily decisions, or specific objectives

These types of work teams allow employees who might not otherwise have the opportunity to contribute their thoughts and ideas to do so. Employees who previously performed only the functions expected of them can now play an integral role in shaping procedures and policies. By becoming a part of a group that is given the authority to make decisions, they can now play a requisite role in improving operations.

Succession planning: Identifying future leaders

It's not new news that the bulk of the population is aging. It's no surprise that the labor pool is shrinking and that it is becoming harder and harder to find talented and qualified employees. What may come as a surprise, though, is the impact that these changes may ultimately have on your organization. In particular, the growing number of employees who will be eligible for retirement in the near future may mean that your ability to fill key positions will be threatened.

A survey conducted by Management Recruiters International, Inc. (MRI), a subsidiary of CDI Corp., indicates that the demand for mid-managers, executives, and professionals continues to be high. Virtually every industry reports critical needs for mid- to upper-level managers and professionals — from 25 percent in the textile industry to 73.9 percent in the printing industry. Demand in the financial services industry is at 55.3 percent, according to the survey.

Worse, research by Development Dimensions International (DDI), a global workforce and leadership training, staffing, and assessment firm based in Bridgeville, Pennsylvania, indicates that companies are at risk to lose a substantial number of their executives within the next five years. "There are going to be between 40 and 50 percent of general managers eligible for retirement in the next five years," says William Byham of DDI. "Most companies aren't ready for retirement from anybody because they don't have the backups. There is a tremendous war for talent."

The impact of these changes is already being felt by many companies.

Whether your replacement needs are the result of tragedy, transition, or trial and error, considering the issue of succession now can help you accomplish these staffing changes smoothly, with minimal disruption to your internal processes and a seamless transition for employees — and customers!

While in the not-so-distant past, organizations were eager to harvest new talent from outside their organizations, today many recognize the value of growing talent from within. Having someone who knows the history of your organization can be valuable in higher level positions — someone who knows the culture, the systems, and the other players will be well prepared when moved into a higher level position. And the positive impact on motivation — both for the promoted worker and for other employees who see that opportunity for advancement is possible — can be substantial.

Too often, though, the talent pool, particularly in smaller companies, may be very shallow, forcing companies to turn outside for talent. This doesn't have to be the case.

Clearly there are advantages to grooming managerial talent from within. But how do you do it?

Identify what skills and competencies are needed

The first step to effective succession planning is clearly identifying the skills and competencies that your organization needs. Some examples of competencies are delegating responsibility, establishing strategic direction, operational decision making, building trust, communications skills, and financial acumen.

The process of identifying competencies can be time consuming, but it is an important first step.

Make sure the direction comes from the top

The impetus for succession planning efforts needs to come from the very top of the organization. It is not unusual for managers to resist succession planning efforts. While managers certainly play an important role in developing employees, they have certain self interests that can get in the way of total commitment. It can be difficult for managers to encourage a good employee to move up the ladder, because it creates a hole in the department as well as uncertainty that the hole can be adequately filled. In addition, individual managers may feel resentful or threatened when their staff members are targeted for development and promotion, while they feel overlooked.

Develop an acceleration pool

How can you identify the employees who are likely to have potential for growth? Look for the people who are quick to accept more responsibility; who want to learn more; who continually ask "What next?"

While keeping your eyes open for natural talent is a good idea, you should also be consciously looking for employees who exhibit the competencies that you have identified. Again, don't overlook the quiet employees. There is often hidden talent lying dormant, just waiting to be discovered.

An acceleration pool — literally, a list of highly skilled, seasoned, and qualified employees — can help ensure that key positions can be filled internally. These individuals are provided with training and job experiences that prepare them to move into more advanced positions. Instead of focusing on just one person for succession to a specific position, the acceleration pool concept provides multiple employees with the experience, education, and training they need to move up within the organization.

Active involvement in skill development is critical. Look around the organization, choose people that have talent, then develop them. Give them a series of experiences that will prepare them for the higher level job. Don't just let chance define who gets those key experiences.

Who is ultimately responsible for an employee's career? The employee. While there are direct benefits to your company in taking a proactive approach to identifying employees with the skills and capabilities your organization will need in the future, you should also expect employees to play an integral role in their own career management.

Keep in mind, though, that not everybody wants more responsibility. There will be a certain percentage of your staff that remains very happy in their current positions.

Be aware, too, that good succession planning assumes that your company is prepared to be honest with employees about their potential. Some employees may simply not be management material. They need to know that. You can't develop everybody; there are a limited number of advancement opportunities in any organization. This doesn't mean that there aren't other opportunities for all employees. There may be opportunities to participate on special projects, or to lead a team or task force, or to learn a new skill. These opportunities can be available to any employee who expresses an interest. And just because an employee isn't identified as a candidate for advancement now, doesn't mean he or she won't be in the future.

Additional resources

The Employee Involvement Association (www.eia.com) is a nonprofit service organization composed of members from finance, commerce, industry, and government sectors, dedicated to the worth, contributions, and benefits of employee suggestion systems and other employee involvement processes. (525 S.W. 5th Street Suite A, Des Moines, Iowa 50309-4501, 515-282-8192.)

10

EDUCATION AND TRAINING

"Higher education and business are basically interdependent. One needs money to produce educated people, and the other needs educated people to produce money."
—Milton Eisenhower

Education and training for employees is not new. In fact, the first program for employee education began in the late 19th century. It was started by the National Cash Register Co. (NCR). In 1894, John H. Patterson, the founder of NCR, set up a school for salesmen at his company's Dayton, Ohio, headquarters. Employees were taught to deliver a proven sales pitch. In 1903, in what may have been the first management training program in the country, Patterson set up a school for top-performing salesmen near Dayton.

In 1926, General Motors Corporation took the step of buying two private management schools. These schools were renamed General Motors Institute. Higher-level management skills such as finance and marketing were taught to supervisors and engineers.

In 1928, Harvard University established the first university program for working managers. That summer, 170 executives spent six weeks studying a condensed version of Harvard's MBA program.

In the 21st century, employee training has exploded as a 2000 study by the American Society for Training and Development (ASTD) of training patterns of organizations around the world shows. The study looked at training practices and expenditures from 501 U.S. organizations and more than 400 organizations from 47 countries outside the U.S.

Overall, employers spent an average of $627 per employee on training in 1998. Expenditures were the highest among respondents in the United States ($724 per employee) and the lowest in Asia ($241 per employee). Comparing 1997 with 1998, The U.S. and Canada both experienced increases in training expenditures per employee (11 percent and 18 percent, respectively). All of the regions experienced increases in training expenditures as a percent of payroll from 1997 to 1998. The largest increase was seen in Canada, where expenditures increased from 1.5 percent in 1997 to 2.3 percent in 1998.

Respondents in every region expected an increase in the percentage of employees receiving training in 1999.

In spite of the proliferation of computer-based and Internet training options, instructor-led classroom training continued to be the predominant form of training delivery in all six regions. A small percentage of training — between 8 percent and 9 percent in most regions — was delivered via learning technologies. However, most respondents continued to project that the learning-technology category will grow significantly in the coming years.

The two technologies used by the largest percentage of respondents to present information to learners were text-only computer-based training (CBT) and multimedia CBT. Over 50 percent of all respondents in all regions (except for multimedia CBT in Japan) used these technologies in 1998. Among the distribution methods, CD-ROM and e-mail were the most commonly used in four of the six regions.

And, says ASTD, investments in training pay off. After a major study of training practices and outcomes of 575 U.S.-based publicly traded firms during 1996, 1997, and 1998, ASTD, with the help of Saba consultants, found that companies that invested $680 more in training per employee than the average company in the study improved their total stockholder return the next year by six percentage points (even after considering other factors).

"It is clear that a firm's commitment to workplace learning is directly linked to its bottom line — and investors, Wall Street, and financial analysts should pay attention," says Mark Van Buren, Director of Research for ASTD. ASTD researchers also found a similar pattern when looking at gross profit margin, income per employee, and price-to-book ratios. "More companies are discovering that training is critical to their success," says Van Buren.

Every year, millions of employees attend continuing education programs offered by private business and associations representing virtually every industry under the sun. In addition, millions more employees receive in-house training from the companies for which they work.

Many factors have caused an increased demand for continuing education — from both corporations and individuals. One of the most important is the increased competition for available jobs. This is due to the baby boom, a greater number of women in the job market, and more and more workers staying on the job past retirement age. Other factors include rapid technological change, especially in the computer and medical fields, and the rising educational level of the population. Finding employees with appropriate qualifications, experience, or "fit" has become more and more difficult, but there are many more un- or under-qualified applicants out there. For small business owners, it will continue to be very difficult to find qualified, competent, and loyal entry-level employees (or employees willing to work for the salary and benefits that small companies can afford to offer). For larger companies, and for higher-end positions in smaller companies, the reverse is true — a large number of employees (many older and quite experienced) are vying for fewer and fewer spots at the top of the corporate ladder. In today's changing job market, offering training to employees to bring their skills up to date can be an essential part of both the employee's career and his or her capability on the job.

Today, countless organizations across the country are finding that education is yet another way to motivate their workers. Courses can be offered to employees at virtually every level of the organization.

Training topics

Training can take place in a number of different topic areas. Some common categories of training are discussed below.

Customer service

Without customers, no business will survive. Recognizing this, as well as the enormous impact that employees have on getting and keeping customers, many companies provide a variety of opportunities for employees to develop and hone their customer service skills.

Technology

Advances in technology are constant, and as these changes occur, employees need to be trained to perform effectively. Companies that provide timely and adequate training for employees find that their staff is not only more competent, but also more comfortable in dealing with the rampant changes around them. Simply presenting a new software program to employees and expecting them to learn it can create stress, frustration, and dissatisfaction.

Interpersonal skills

Today's employees rarely work independently. They are part of teams that cross departmental — and even organizational — boundaries. Add to this the increasingly diverse work environment with employees representing a wide range of ages, nationalities, beliefs, and backgrounds. The need for good communication skills is critical. Training programs that focus on conflict management, dealing with difficult people, communicating effectively, and respecting differences are more and more common.

Quality improvement

A plethora of quality initiatives with catchy titles points to the fact that many organizations are involving employees in massive training efforts as a way of improving product and service quality.

Technical skills

Employees need to remain up-to-date on changes in their careers. Technical skills training can run the gamut from seminars on accounting practices, to updates on legal standards, to management training and skills-based learning in a variety of fields. Technical-skills training is probably the broadest form of continuing education offered.

The benefits of employee education

Why is training a motivator? Many employees aspire to self-improvement and advancement — whether that means more responsibility in the job they currently have, or the opportunity to apply for, and receive, a promotion to a higher-level job. Education and training are major factors in providing employees with the knowledge they need in order to move on in their careers.

The training itself can also be motivating. Employees who belong to professional organizations enjoy the opportunity to network with colleagues, to hear presentations by experts in their fields, or even to speak at these sessions themselves.

Often training is looked upon as a benefit or perk by employees. While on-line training opportunities are becoming more prevalent, the hands-on attributes of in-person training (as well as the opportunity for a few days off work, perhaps in an attractive destination) can be very attractive to employees.

Training offers benefits to employers as well. Well-trained employees are more productive and efficient; they perform more effectively and make fewer errors. Because they feel more competent, they tend to have more positive attitudes toward themselves — and their jobs.

Training can be an important part of a succession-planning program. With an aging population driven by the large number of baby boomers who will soon be retiring from the workforce, succession planning has become a critical issue for many organizations. By identifying employees with potential to move into higher-level positions and providing them with the appropriate training and education, both employer and employee benefit.

Employee education offers many benefits, including improved attitudes, increased knowledge and skill, higher productivity, improved profitability, better employee morale, and improved company image.

Through education, employees can also achieve promotions, personal growth, and a sense of satisfaction.

But not all training offers the same benefits. Training sessions can be enjoyable and productive, or they can be boring and a waste of time. Whether you're training your employees through CBT (computer-based training), in-house programs, or attendance at public seminars, you want to make sure that they're getting the best training possible.

Types of training

The three primary methods of offering training to employees include: in-house training, public seminars, and computer-based training.

In-house training

There are several types of in-house training, ranging from supervisory coaching of employees to actual training seminars. Other options include informal discussion groups and self-development through computer-assisted instruction or videotape. The human resource or training department plays a major role in any of these areas. Our focus here will be on in-house seminars.

For any in-house training program to work effectively, it is important to have top-management support. To get this support, the training personnel need to demonstrate a need for training, do a good job of developing trial programs, and show proof of a positive result.

The two major objections will be the time and expense that training entails. The response to these objections should address the time and expense wasted by untrained staff.

Once support is achieved and you're on your way to a formal training effort, the following factors are important:

> ➤ A central authority must carry out and monitor the training process.

> ➤ The role of the central authority should be clearly defined.

> ➤ Managers and supervisors must participate from the beginning. They will need to be convinced of the importance of training. They will also need to understand the important role they have in the success of this training.

- ► An information campaign should be instituted. Employees must know about the training opportunities the company is offering. Training needs to be promoted as a positive aspect of employment.

- ► Initial training efforts should be aimed at areas that are ripe for training.

- ► Supervisors should be encouraged to talk about courses with subordinates before training begins.

- ► Employees going through training should complete end-of-course action plans to help use the techniques and skills learned.

- ► Follow-up training must be provided to help further the learning process and encourage retention.

- ► Managers and supervisors should aid in the design of training.

- ► Employee response to training must be continually monitored.

The major advantage of having in-house training is the time allowed for the development of training programs that are specific to employee needs. In addition, there is the opportunity to monitor training results on an on-going basis. Training structures can be modified as necessary.

If, however, your company is too small, or management simply will not support the development of in-house training, there is another option you can explore. You can look into public seminars.

Choosing outside training

The ability to receive training over the Internet hasn't caused a drop in the number of public seminars offered to businesses. In fact, the field has grown tremendously over the past several years, with both private companies and trade associations presenting a myriad of public offerings every day.

Because there is such a wide variation in the type, content, and quality of these offerings, it is important to know what to look for — and what to look out for — when considering these opportunities.

The topic

When an employee comes to you with a brochure on a seminar, there's no doubt that the first thing you look for is the topic. Is it something that would benefit the company? Is it related to the job being done? Will it provide the information needed? These are just a few of the questions you ask as you look at the title and outline. For many business people, the topic is one of the most important factors in the decision of whether to send an employee to a program.

Another important consideration will be whether a live seminar is the best way for the employee to learn this particular topic. Is the topic something that could be better taught internally, or more efficiently learned in some other manner (i.e., videotape, computer-based training, books, etc.)?

Speakers

No matter how well the topic fits your needs, you won't want to send an employee to a seminar unless you can be sure that the speakers have something worthwhile to offer. Have you heard of the people speaking at the program? What are their reputations? What comments have you heard about them from others? It's a simple matter to check credentials and background information on-line, if only to find comments from past attendees. It's worth the effort to gather as much information as possible.

Sponsor

A flashy brochure doesn't guarantee a quality presentation. If you're not familiar with the sponsor of a program you've heard about, you should try to gather some information before signing anyone up for the program. Call and request names of prior attendees you can use for references. Ask around. Has anyone you know attended any program sponsored by this organization? What was his or her impression? Again, consider sources of on-line information.

Level of the program

The level of the program will affect your overall impression. Even if someone has been in a particular field for several years, they may need to attend a basic program introducing an innovation or technical change. If an employee is new to a job, but has very high technical knowledge, an intermediate program may be what you're looking for.

Handout materials

Only a certain amount of learning can take place in a lecture situation. Many seminar attendees prefer seminars that provide high-quality materials they will be able to use as a reference after the program — binders, books, CDs, and videotapes are all ways in which learning can be continued (and shared!) after the live seminar.

Format

What will be the style of presentation? Will it be a lecture format? Workshop? One-on-one? Will there be one speaker? A panel? A series of short lectures? Format considerations vary with individual preference and, of course, the topic of discussion. For each seminar you consider, you should ask, "Is this the best format for getting the information?"

Time/cost

The cost of a program goes beyond the price in the brochure. It also includes the price of travel and accommodations and the price of an employee's time away from the office. Take all of these costs into consideration before deciding whether a seminar will be worthwhile.

Location

Location is also a consideration. An attractive location is an added incentive for employees. If quality is lacking, however, the company may not be getting much value from the employee's experience.

Computer-based training

Sometimes the traditional, one-on-one training structures are simply not suitable to your needs. Consider the following examples:

► You have 3500 employees in 70 locations. You're introducing a new product or a new program. You need to train 2500 of these employees right away. How can you possibly get it all done?

► You've been conducting employee orientation on a monthly basis for several years. With turnover remaining constant, you really don't see an end in sight. It wouldn't be so bad if you could just use the same material from month to month, but it seems that you're constantly updating, changing, and adding to the information. Isn't there a better way?

➤ You'd like to go back to school to pursue your master's degree, but you just don't have the time — or the flexibility — to participate in a traditional university program.

Training costs and training demands are increasing exponentially. As employers compete for an ever-shrinking number of skilled workers, and as free time becomes increasingly precious, alternatives to traditional training and education have become more of a necessity than a luxury. And, luckily, as bandwidth becomes less of a scarce resource and more and more companies are becoming networked, the move to training using Internet, intranet, or extranet technology is a growing option.

Today, many employees have access to Internet-based training right at their work stations. Those who don't can often take advantage of the training through computer labs or computer kiosks provided by the organization.

The benefits of online learning? According to those who have experienced computer-based training, the benefits include saving money on training (including reductions in travel costs and employee time away from the office), more convenient access to last-minute training and information, and the ability to easily and inexpensively update information so that it is immediately accessible to any number of employees in any number of locations.

Marie Raines is a performance consultant with BusinessWorks, Inc. in Richardson, Texas, a company that creates learning solutions for businesses by using interactive multimedia technology. Raines points to a number of benefits provided by Internet-based training. Participants can —

➤ view enjoyable interactive business-learning presentations at their desktops, in synchronized full-color and full-motion video, audio, text, and slides;

➤ work at their own pace — log on and off at will, or pick up where they left off if they need to exit prior to completion;

➤ navigate or search topics, slides, or text at any time in the program;

- track, test, and report users' progress and scores to verify learning results; and

- customize projects with video characters, graphics, and illustrations to add to the interactivity and increase learning and retention of information.

Employees can enter a virtual classroom at their convenience. They can be participating in a group, yet doing so independently. Internet-based training can be especially useful when you have only one person to train. No longer do you have to worry about having enough critical mass for a class.

A major advantage to Internet-based training and one that offers endless opportunity is its ability to allow interaction between learner and instructor.

There are some barriers, however. The primary potential barrier is your existing computer system and system support. Depending on where you are in your adoption of technology, it may be an easy thing for you to do, or you may need to purchase a service and hire someone to keep the system managed and maintained.

Another barrier involves accommodation to the transition from face-to-face learning to learning in an electronic environment. However, experts and those who have participated in these activities claim the transition is a relatively easy one to make, and affirm that the new environment offers its own benefits.

Some topics are simply not suitable for online learning. Dr. Jo Ann Oravec, who has pioneered online learning at the University of Wisconsin-Whitewater, says that "classes that include topics such as 'how to conduct a face-to-face meeting' should have sufficient on-campus time so that students can explore these topics with suitable role-playing exercises."

She adds, though, that "as videoconferencing technologies become more sophisticated, even some of these sessions can be simulated online."

You also need to consider more than the computers that your employees will be using. Peripheral equipment — such as printers — are also critical considerations. You'll want to ensure that employees can print material that may contain graphics or fonts that your current printers may not be equipped to handle.

Many vendors now make online learning programs available. They can be located through an Internet search or by contacting companies that currently handle some of your training needs.

Getting a Degree Online

Remember when pursuing a degree meant attending classes at a nearby university? Your program options were limited by the classes offered within convenient driving distance, and by your ability to balance your life and work schedule with the timing of courses offered?

Well, that was then and this is now. More and more working professionals are taking advantage of the opportunities presented by online degree programs like the MBA program offered by the University of Wisconsin-Whitewater.

Jo Ann Oravec is the author of *Virtual Individuals, Virtual Groups: Human Dimensions of Groupware and Computer Networking*, and is an assistant professor of business and economics at the University of Wisconsin at Whitewater. She is a strong proponent of online learning, and says, "Online learning will soon be a major force in certain kinds of education: graduate education, especially at the MBA level, is one of these. Online classrooms will become popular because students will simply demand to have more choices for education.

"For people with demanding and erratic work schedules and considerable responsibilities at home, such flexible learning provides a tremendous opportunity."

Mastery of the online world can also have benefits on the job, as Oravec points out. "People who engage in extensive online interaction at work and also participate in online classroom exchanges are likely to become more skillful in both realms, using insights and strategies gained from their workplace interactions in their educational activities — and vice versa.

"I've found many of my students to be very much at ease with corresponding with me online. They asked questions about classroom material and provided interesting perspectives that we did not have time to cover in class."

Other training opportunities

There are a number of other training opportunities that even the smallest company with the most modest budget can take advantage of. Consider the following options.

Brown-bag lunches

Invite employees to bring a lunch to a conference room or breakroom for presentations given by other staff members. Ask an effective manager to share management tips with his or her colleagues. Ask an employee who is a whiz at a certain task to share his or her expertise with others.

Reading groups

Select a book (on a management topic, a specific industry topic, etc.) and ask interested employees to read it, then gather to discuss what they learned. This can be done chapter by chapter or an entire book at a time. Ask for volunteers from among staff members to lead the process.

Discussion groups

Do you have a group of employees who are interested in a particular topic? Give them the opportunity to get together to discuss the issue and learn from each other in the process. Select a volunteer facilitator to lead the discussion. Ask for topic suggestions from staff members.

Special assignments

Special project assignments can be wonderful learning experiences. Employees will be motivated because they were selected for the task, as well as by the task itself. Learning occurs on the job and is most effective if a skilled mentor can help to facilitate the process.

Mentoring

Speaking of mentors, a mentoring program can be a great way to match up seasoned employees with new hires or less experienced staff members. The experience is motivating for both parties.

Community events

Chambers of Commerce, technical colleges, universities, libraries, and some private businesses offer training and education — often at no cost — to local businesses.

Training pays

The payoffs for training and development are proven, not only in terms of improving talent and skills to boost productivity, but also in terms of attracting and retaining that talent. To further investigate how companies are using training and development to attract and retain their employees, ASTD and the Society for Human Resource Management (SHRM) conducted a benchmarking study to look at how organizations use employee growth and career initiatives to find and keep employees.

Seven companies, called Exemplary Practice Partners, were screened and chosen to participate in the study. The companies included Dow Chemical Company, Edward Jones, Great Plains, LensCrafters, Inc., Sears, Roebuck & Company, Southwest Airlines, and South African Breweries. In comparison with the ASTD Benchmarking Service database, in which training investment data is kept for over 2,500 organizations worldwide, these seven companies —

- ▶ trained more employees and gave training-eligible employees more hours of training;

- ▶ spent less per employee, but more as a percentage of payroll on employee training;

- ▶ delivered training more often using learning technologies and less via the classroom;

- ▶ spent more on technology as a percentage of the training budget;

- ▶ utilized more outside resources to provide training;

- ▶ spent less on outside providers of training; and

- ▶ engaged, more often, in the use of compensation practices, work practices, training practices, and human performance management practices.

Additionally, each of these seven companies experiences lower turnover rates and higher employee satisfaction than the average company in its industry. These seven companies believe that this is due in large part to the investments they make in their people, through fair and equitable HR policies and practices, and in their employee growth and career development initiatives.

What would it take for your company to realize these benefits? The study found the following similarities among these firms:

- ► Each company made employees responsible for their own development, while simultaneously providing them with generous support (and accountability) from managers, leaders, coaches, mentors, and teams.

- ► The organizations supported training from the very highest levels, realizing that building the knowledge capacity of their workers is a necessary strategy for business success.

- ► Each company has a strong identity and culture in which employees are understood to be one of the main reasons for the success of the businesses.

- ► Organizational infrastructures were put in place to support HR efforts to attract and retain employees. This was enabled by the use of technology.

The payoffs for recognizing and responding to employee development needs are substantial. Higher motivation. Reduced turnover. Increased productivity. Employees want to learn and grow in their jobs. Providing the education, training, and resources your staff needs to improve their skills and knowledge not only meets their needs — it meets your needs as well.

11

HEALTH AND
WELLNESS PROGRAMS

One in six U.S. employees is so overworked that he or she is unable to use up annual vacation time, despite the fact that Americans have the least vacation time in the industrialized world, according to a study sponsored by Oxford Health Plans, Inc.

Of the 632 men and women participating in the survey, 34 percent report they have such pressing jobs that they have no down time at work. Another 32 percent indicate that they work and eat lunch at the same time, 32 percent say they never leave the building once they arrive at work, 19 percent say their job makes them feel older than they are, and 17 percent say work causes them to lose sleep.

Many companies are responding to the increasing stresses of the workplace with health and wellness programs that are offered to employees as employee benefits.

A 1999 Worksite Health Promotion Survey by William M. Mercer and the Association for Worksite Health Promotion showed that health promotion programs became more prevalent in the past decade, with nine of ten worksites sponsoring at least one health-promoting activity.

Rising health-care costs and other pressures are likely to contribute to further expansion of these programs. Not surprisingly, the survey found that the most common reason that employers sponsor health-promotion programs is to keep workers healthy — this reason is cited by 84 percent of the 1,544 survey participants. Other reasons cited frequently include improving employee morale (77 percent), reducing health-care costs (76 percent), and retaining good employees (75 percent).

Health promotion can encompass a range of programs, including —

➤ formal health and safety policies,

➤ health screenings and risk assessments,

➤ injury prevention,

➤ awareness education,

➤ lifestyle behavior change,

➤ demand management (through self-care books, nurse advice lines, etc.),

➤ disease management (for back pain, diabetes, depression, asthma, etc.), and

➤ on-site fitness centers.

The survey found a strong association between the presence of health as an explicit corporate mission or value and a higher incidence of all types of health promotion programs, stronger evaluation efforts, higher participation, and fewer perceived barriers to program success.

At least two out of every five companies have health-awareness programs, according to a benefits survey by the Administrative Management Society. Of the 305 companies surveyed, close to half (42 percent) have formal health, physical fitness, or recreational programs. About 54 percent said they did not have such programs, while 4 percent are seriously considering them.

Job pressures impact health and wellness

The price of success is high. It takes its toll upon today's workers in the form of ulcers, heart attacks, high blood pressure, and other physical ailments. Other symptoms include lethargy, irritability, and fatigue. Along with these nagging physical problems, employees often feel dissatisfaction with their jobs and may ultimately quit. This type of turnover is often blamed on burnout.

Consider the following examples:

Sally is a nurse in a large hospital. Her hours are irregular. She deals daily with life and death situations. She must always be on her toes, ready to make quick decisions. She's been a nurse for the past 15 years. During the last two years, she has found it harder and harder to go to work. And, once at work, she's been making some minor mistakes — mistakes that may be affecting her future with the hospital.

Marsha is a copywriter. She says she really enjoys her work. She adds, however, "The deadlines can really drive you crazy. A lot of little things can really add up so you want to give up the whole works. Right now I love it — but I couldn't do this for the rest of my life."

Sally and Marsha are both suffering from job burnout. Although they're at different stages of the burnout process, their symptoms are quite similar. Burnout is a debilitating psychological condition brought about by unrelieved work stress. Burnout results in —

▶ lowered energy reserves, exhaustion, and loss of enthusiasm,

▶ increased susceptibility to illness,

▶ dissatisfaction and pessimism, and

▶ increased absenteeism and inefficiency at work.

The causes of burnout are many. Often it is the result of a work situation in which the person gets the feeling that he or she is beating his or her head against the wall day after day. It can result from boring work (boredom can cause burnout very quickly), lack of feedback, over-commitment, lack of recognition, unrealized self-expectations, or job pressure. There are four kinds of job pressure: too much work, pressure from superiors, deadlines, and low salaries.

Studies of burnout victims show these people to be hard working, dedicated, and idealistic. They are often a company's most valued workers; they are people who set high standards for themselves. For these employees, burnout can cause high blood pressure, family problems, and other difficulties. From the employer's point of view, burnout can cause low productivity, increased absenteeism, and high turnover.

Job burnout is closely related to job stress. Every day, thousands of North Americans go home from work with nagging headaches, tense muscles, back problems, and other physical ailments. When they get home, many of them must deal with more problems that try their patience and make them irritable.

What are they experiencing? Stress. Stress lowers productivity. Statistics from the U.S. Clearinghouse for Mental Health show that the U.S. loses $17 billion in productivity annually due to stress. Other studies report even higher figures. Many employers have found that prevention can be far less costly than the lost productivity, errors, and accidents associated with stress.

How jobs contribute to stress

The first important consideration for employers is an awareness of the causes of stress. A number of factors can cause a job situation to be stressful:

- ► *The job itself:* This includes too much or too little work, poor physical working conditions, and time pressures.

- ► *The employee's role in the organization:* Employees may have problems with role conflict or confusion, responsibility for people, or lack of participation in decision making.

- ► *The employee's career development:* This may involve under- or over-promotion, lack of job security, or unmet ambition.

- ► *The organizational structure and climate:* This factor involves lack of effective consultation, restrictions on behavior, and office politics.

- ► *The relationships within the organization:* If an employee has poor relationships with the boss, poor relationships with colleagues and subordinates, or difficulties in delegating responsibility, stress will be the result.

- ► *Any extra-organizational sources:* Problems can arise over company versus family demands, or company versus the employee's own interests.

- ► *Any personality conflicts with management:* Managers may have an effect on an employee's ability to cope with change, motivation, and behavioral patterns. This depends on individual employees and individual personality traits.

Some jobs are more stressful than others. Jobs that tend to be most stressful are those in which employees have little or no control over the work they do — laborers or secretaries, for instance. The more control that can be built into an employee's job, the less stressful the job will become.

How do you know when stress is getting to your workforce?

There are many danger signs, including lack of interest and enthusiasm, low morale, high turnover, absenteeism, tension, low productivity, high number of accidents, lack of cooperation, impulsive decision making, negative attitude or cynicism, disregard for high priority tasks, inappropriate humor, poor interpersonal relationships, high anxiety, depression, and boredom.

The benefits to the employer of recognizing and taking steps to deal with the effects of stress are many. They include —

► higher employee morale,

► enhanced team spirit,

► improved decision making,

► decreases in absenteeism and turnover, and

► decreases in insurance expenses/medical costs.

Productivity and motivation are becoming major concerns for employers throughout the country. Both job stress and job burnout take a physical and emotional toll on the workforce. More and more employers are trying to fight the problem before it becomes a problem. One way to do this is to introduce programs and practices designed to decrease stress and improve wellness.

Creating a low-stress environment

As an employer, there are many simple things you can do to establish a low-stress environment. Here are some examples:

► Ensure that job requirements are reasonably demanding. Both too-high expectations and too-low expectations can create stress. Employees need to be challenged, but not overwhelmed.

► Provide opportunities for continued growth. If employees stop learning, they feel as though they are stagnating. That is how burnout develops. Consider methods of keeping your employees interested in their jobs. Consider providing them with opportunities to continue learning through cross-training, attendance at seminars, and new responsibilities.

➤ Involve employees in decision making. As we've already seen, employees like to be involved. By giving employees the opportunity to participate in decision making, they develop feelings of control over their work and their futures. Lack of control is one of the largest contributing factors in the development of burnout.

➤ Provide ample recognition and support. We've talked about this at length already, but it bears repeating. You can never offer too much praise, as long as it's sincere.

➤ Help employees to see the value in what they do. It is important that your employees see their jobs as contributing to the big picture. They need to know that what they do matters and that what you do as a company is important and valuable. In short, they need to feel good about themselves and what they do. That's what motivation is all about.

Simple tasks. But, like many other employers, you'll probably find that the results of these simple changes can be positive both in terms of intangible benefits (like improved morale and company commitment) and tangible benefits (like decreased health costs and increased productivity).

The benefits of health and wellness programs

Stress has been called the black lung of the technical class. Fortunately, employers are beginning to understand the connection between mental performance and physical fitness. There are many indications that employee wellness programs really do decrease absenteeism and may also increase productivity.

Many firms have started wellness programs. These programs offer employees a positive way to stay healthy and help resolve problems that might interfere with work.

Heart disease, cancer, and accidents are the leading causes of death for people under 65. These same problems drag down a company's productivity. Fortunately, more and more companies are finding that these health problems can be curbed by eliminating smoking, ensuring proper exercise and diet, and controlling high blood pressure.

In addition to combating physical problems, wellness plans also respond to other employees' interests. Often this results in improved morale and greater employee loyalty to the company.

In Sweden, it has been official policy for nearly 40 years to move non-active workers into more active roles. Studies in Sweden have shown that industrial exercise programs lead to fewer sick days and fewer hospital admissions.

Dr. Roy J.Shephard, professor of preventive medicine and director of the University of Toronto School of Physical and Health Education, conducted a study of the staff of two insurance companies in Toronto during the 1980s. He used the North American Life Assurance Co. as his control group for comparison with the Canada Life Assurance Co.

The Canada Life people met three times weekly for 30-minute sessions to do exercises that included rhythmic calisthenics, jogging, and games to increase endurance and cardiovascular fitness. They met for six months. Among the employees who worked out at least twice a week, turnover dropped from 15 percent to 1.5 percent and absenteeism fell 22 percent. The majority of those who exercised regularly realized "substantial gains in conventional measures of fitness, such as body fat, aerobic power, and flexibility."

Tenneco, a large energy-related company in Houston, has also had great success with its health and fitness program. Tenneco's health and fitness program initially had six main objectives:

► To increase the level of employees' cardiovascular fitness

► To increase employees' knowledge of positive health habits and reduce coronary risk factors

► To obtain employee ownership in the program and promote self-responsibility

► To motivate employees to improve and/or maintain their optimum standards of health

► To further develop the above objectives with interested Tenneco divisions outside the Houston area

> ▶ To further develop program adherence by involving the employees' support groups (families, friends, and peers)

Tenneco's program was chosen as the top corporate program in 1984 by both the Washington Business Group on Health and the Association for Fitness in Business.

Wellness programs became popular in the 1970s and 1980s. These programs continue to be popular today, and studies continue to show that they are valued by employees.

According to a survey sponsored by Oxford Health Plans, Inc., while only 29 percent of the companies surveyed provided healthy lunches or dinners, a full 84 percent of employees took advantage of the benefit when it was offered. Similarly, only 18 percent of the companies surveyed offered membership to a health club either on the premises or off-site, but when they did, 72 percent of the employees joined.

The survey indicated that 13 percent of employers offered a meditation room for their employees, and 55 percent of these employees participated. Only six percent of employers offered massage services to their employees, and 60 percent of these employees took advantage of the benefit.

"Our findings show that these perks should no longer be considered alternatives, but are mainstays, since they are well-accepted among workers and demonstrate an employer's commitment to promoting wellness in the workplace," says Alan Muney, M.D., chief medical officer and executive vice president at Oxford.

Interest in these benefits showed variation by age. Younger workers (age 18 to 34) were more likely than their older colleagues (age 35 to 44 and 45 to 54) to take advantage of the fitness club membership. Older workers were also less likely to eat healthy lunches or dinners than their younger counterparts (when healthy food was offered, 88 percent of those age 18 to 34 took advantage of the offer; 92 percent of those age 35 to 55, 80 percent of those 45 to 50, and 70 percent of those 55 and older).

The most likely to take advantage of massage, however, were older baby boomers (when offered, 100 percent of workers age 45 to 54 took advantage; 60 percent of those age 18 to 34).

Steps to an effective program

If you've considered the establishment of a health and wellness program, there are several important keys to success:

- ► Involve top management. In order for wellness programs to work effectively, top management must be involved and supportive. A company must commit adequate money and staff to meet the goals of the program. Company leaders should visibly support the program through their own participation.

- ► Designate responsibility. Designate someone to be responsible for the program. It's important that responsibility is centered in one area and coordinated by one person. That person is very often someone in the human resources department. A company may also choose to establish a committee to help oversee the program. Committee members may include representatives from human resources, employee health, communications/marketing, as well as line staff. Through the committee, the company is able to determine the needs and interests of employees, develop a plan, recruit program participants, and implement and evaluate the program.

- ► Determine the need. Conduct a survey to determine employee interest. This survey can be prepared very simply by the planning committee and distributed through inter-office mail. You're looking for two things: an indication of the level of interest in employer-sponsored wellness, and an indication of the areas of interest among employees. For example, your particular employee group might not be interested in a quit-smoking program (maybe very few employees smoke), but they would be interested in company-sponsored aerobics. You won't know unless you give them the opportunity to tell you. Some companies use specially designed survey forms called health risk appraisals. These appraisals can be computer analyzed (some are even available on-line) and provide in-depth health information to both employees and management.

- ► Identify resources. Determine company and community resources. Many communities have access to services through local health care organizations and associations like the American Heart Association that work with corporations to promote healthy lifestyles. Your first step is to determine what type of support is already available in your community. Then, you need to present this information to management and ask for some commitment of funds, space, and time for developing a program. It's important that you know what your resources are before you begin planning.

➤ When identifying available resources, consider existing health services (including health screening), existing facilities (including community services), the skills and talents of employees, available community options such as free information about wellness, fee-for-service providers, and consultants experienced in the design, implementation, and evaluation of such programs. Perhaps your company is not large enough to fund a full-scale health-care program. Many companies aren't, but there are still ways to provide wellness benefits to employees. A company on a very small budget needs only to provide room to move around and a place to change clothes. Expensive exercise equipment is not essential. However, good training people are essential. One of the most common options chosen by companies that cannot accommodate a program on their premises is the company-paid or partially paid membership in a local health club or YMCA.

➤ Establish objectives. As with any endeavor, it's important to have specific goals to work toward as a group. These goals could be something like a certain percentage of all employees participating in the program, or specific health-maintenance concerns such as weight loss, lowered blood pressure, or decrease in number of employees who smoke. Your goals should be jointly established by employees and the committee, and progress toward these goals should be communicated on a regular basis. You should choose goals that can be monitored to evaluate the program. You should also assist employees in setting realistic personal goals. Offer incentives for goal achievement. The employee sets the goal and develops his or her own individual program, but the employer participates by encouraging the employee in his or her endeavors and offering various perks (time off, gift certificates, etc.) for reaching pre-established goals.

➤ Conduct individual health assessments. Each employee who chooses to participate in the program should be assessed before the onset of the program. Whether you do this on-site (through a company nurse, etc.) or through outside providers, it's important that employees get a clean bill of health before they embark on any form of health program.

▶ Monitor effectiveness. Finally, you will want to be able to monitor the effectiveness of the program itself. You'll need to consider employee participation, drop-out rates, and changes in employee health knowledge, attitudes, and behavior. You'll also want to look at long-term effectiveness in terms of decreased absenteeism, use of health-care benefits, number of accidents, and increases in productivity.

Employee assistance programs (EAPs)

For several months, almost everyone on the staff of XYZ Corporation has been aware that Joe is having personal problems. Not only has his personal appearance declined, but he is calling in sick more and more often, especially on Mondays after payday, doing very little work on the days he does show up, and rapidly becoming snappy and irritable. After several complaints from coworkers (and a few from disgruntled customers), Joe's supervisor, Sharon, is beginning to suspect that Joe has a drinking problem.

Working with troubled employees can be one of the most challenging and frustrating aspects of managerial jobs. To ease this process, many organizations have established formal programs to help managers and their employees. Employee Assistance Programs, or EAPs, are systems that provide professional services to employees whose job performance is or may become adversely affected by any number of factors, including substance abuse, emotional problems, family difficulties, legal issues, physical health disorders, and/or similar personal problems. These problems not only threaten the employee's effectiveness on the job, but also tend to trigger a wide range of health problems (physical and emotional), as well as disrupting the performance of other employees.

EAPs can be either on-site, staffed by trained counselors, or, as is most often the case, off-site and accessible to a number of companies and their employees. EAPs provide assistance by using resources already available in the community: attorneys, marriage counselors, addiction counselors, financial counselors, psychologists, and so on.

Employees may be referred to the EAP by their supervisor or manager or may use self-referral. Managers who use EAPs to help their employees deal with problems are not prying. Their concern is bringing the employee's job performance back up to standard. All interaction of an employee with an EAP is confidential.

EAPs aren't new. In fact, in 1917 Macy's Department Store established a program to help employees deal with their personal problems. However, while earlier programs had a focus that was almost exclusively on alcoholism and drug-related problems, today's programs take a more holistic approach and focus on every aspect of the employee's life. The result has been a greater recognition of the fact that everyone is susceptible to problems that can create on-the-job stress, and that the presence of these problems is not a stigma. Consequently, today's programs are more successful because they are more often utilized.

EAPs are based on the philosophy that employees are a valuable company resource that needs to be protected. Employee retention is one of the most notable results of an EAP. Today's EAP is not just for employees; EAPs also serve the employee's family members, corporations, and communities. Today, they are focused more on intervention and prevention, rather than the crisis-oriented approach utilized when they first came into being.

EAPs give employees a confidential outlet for personal or job concerns. They are a way to help maintain existing staff retention and productivity levels by intervening before problems have a negative impact on job situations and morale.

Managers and EAPs

If an employee came to your office and confided in you that he or she was having marital problems, and you responded, "Unless it affects your performance on the job, your personal life doesn't interest me," what do you think would happen? Chances are, word would get around the company very quickly, and you'd probably be looked upon by employees and coworkers as a poor manager.

But suppose you decided to spend some time working with that employee, helping him or her over the problems, counseling the employee during work hours, and being available after hours to empathize and lend a shoulder to lean on. Now what do you think would happen?

Chances are, word would get around the company very quickly, and you'd probably be looked upon by employees and coworkers as a poor manager.

Hard to believe? Let's take a look at a typical situation.

You're the manager of a five-person department. One of your employees confides in you that he's having marital problems. Pete feels a separation is imminent, but he doesn't want anyone else to know about it. You promise to keep his situation confidential. He gets in the habit of stopping in to talk to you for 15 minutes or an hour almost every day.

Of course, the other four people in your department don't know why this employee is suddenly receiving preferential treatment. They begin to complain among themselves and others in the company that Pete is favored. You are spending a great deal of time with him, and you've overlooked the fact that he's been late to work twice in the past week.

Pete's situation isn't getting any better with your counsel. His work is not improving. Your other employees are not being helped by this situation. Their work is not improving. For that matter, you are not being helped by this situation: your work is not improving either.

By spending extra time with an employee to work out personal problems, you are —

- ► increasing the probability that you will be charged with favoritism,

- ► taking your valuable time away from the job your company is paying you to do,

- ► taking the troubled employee's valuable time away from the job your company is paying him or her to do, and

- ► taking other employees' valuable time away from the job your company is paying them to do (because they're now busy gossiping and complaining about your non-work-related relationship with the troubled employee).

The bottom line? You've damaged productivity and morale. And that's exactly what you set out to improve.

Professional distance must be maintained by supervisors. Managers cannot be effective counselors, and trying to do so will only be detrimental to such areas as employee relations and performance evaluation.

EAPs allow companies to deal with personal problems indirectly. Company time is not used to counsel troubled employees. Issues of favoritism are not raised. And, perhaps most important, the employee in question receives qualified professional help — help that can make a difference.

The supervisor's function in the EAP process is threefold:

1) Provide information

2) Encourage the use of EAPs

3) Refer troubled employees

Even this limited involvement, however, can cause problems for managers. There are a number of natural barriers that managers have in referring employees to EAPs:

> *Reluctance to get involved:* If a manager notices that an employee is becoming more and more withdrawn at work, he or she may hesitate to approach that employee. The manager may feel that it is inappropriate to discuss a personal problem with an employee.

> *Reluctance to interfere:* Many times, an employee's problem may not seem to directly affect performance. The manager may not want to interfere unless the issue is directly work-related. The consequence may be, however, that the problem does ultimately affect performance.

> *Reluctance to insult people:* We've been taught to remain politely distant, especially in the workplace. Approaching an employee who we suspect may have a personal problem may seem to us like the ultimate insult.

> *Bite-the-bullet mentality:* We're taught as managers to be proactive. If an employee's work performance is declining due to personal problems, we may think to help only because the work has to get done.

> *Desire to be nice:* Many managers want to be perceived as agreeable. An employee who is consistently late to work because of child-care problems, for example, may receive our empathy and understanding. We may overlook the possibility that this employee may benefit from a visit to an EAP.

▶ *Lack of time:* Face it: Most managers are strapped for time. Once they begin to become involved with the personal problems of employees, that time is at an even greater premium.

Let's take a further look at Joe's problem and Sharon's reaction to illustrate the five phases that a manager may go through before finally making the decision to refer an employee to an EAP:

1) *Uncertainty/denial:* As we have seen, Sharon suspects that Joe is abusing alcohol. But when she approaches Joe, she receives a litany of excuses: "I've had car problems, family problems, marital problems." Sharon makes the decision that she doesn't want to get involved, and Joe promises that it won't happen again. Sharon chooses to minimize the severity of the problem.

2) *Anger, frustration, exasperation:* Time passes and Joe continues to show up late. In addition, his performance has become more sporadic and his temper even shorter. Sharon still doesn't want to get involved, even though she's becoming more and more frustrated. She knows Joe has a lot of family problems. She wants to be nice, and she doesn't want to insult Joe by implying that he can't handle his own personal life.

3) *Guilt, self-doubt, and biting the bullet:* At this stage, Sharon begins to question her own ability to deal with the situation. At the same time, she feels guilty and inadequate. Joe's behavior is continuing to slide downward, and now, in addition, the morale of the other workers in the department is declining and they're beginning to grumble about preferential treatment. It's inventory time, and everyone has to work harder to pull up Joe's slack. Sharon begins to have more frequent confrontations with Joe and is spending too much of her time away from her duties as supervisor. But because she is so busy, Sharon feels she really can't spare the time right now to deal directly with Joe's problem.

4) *Recognition:* Sharon finally realizes that the efforts she's been making have not worked. She knows she needs to try a different course of action and, at this point, begins to consider the corporation's EAP as a possible solution. In order to be able to discuss the situation with Joe to everyone's best advantage, she finds out as much as she can about the EAPs available and talks to a EAP coordinator.

5) *Referral:* Sharon finally confronts Joe. After some argument, Joe admits, "I know I've been slipping, but I've been having some personal problems." Sharon responds by saying, "I understand how personal problems can affect your performance. While it's not my role to become involved in your personal life, I would like to refer you to the company EAP." Joe agrees. Sharon continues to keep notes on Joe's performance and is pleased to find that his work subsequently improves.

Managers need to understand what the EAP entails in some de-tail — how it affects you and your staff individually. Remember, as a supervisor you are looking for increased job performance. You shouldn't need to know what the employee's specific problem is. When you confront a troubled employee, you don't want to talk about his or her personal life. You want to talk about job performance and how problems are exhibited on the job. While some employees may choose to confide in their managers, you must refrain from serving as counselor — you are not trained for this, and intervening in this manner goes beyond your role as manager.

It's also important for managers to remember that one of their major responsibilities is to document performance on the job and offers of help through EAP referral. You can't trust to memory the important facts that signaled a decline in performance. You should make a concerted effort to document any unusual occurrence, such as accidents, absences, missed meetings, or missed deadlines. Too often, supervisors can't remember when a decline in performance began. Your documentation should include —

- ➤ name of employee,
- ➤ date of incident,
- ➤ explanation of the incident,
- ➤ names of others involved,
- ➤ action taken, and
- ➤ whether or not you had a discussion with the employee.

Be sure to document immediately after the incident. Don't rely on your memory to record the event later. Remember, you should be documenting only facts — observable, verifiable behaviors — not rumors, speculations, or guesses.

Cathy Pierzina, a counselor with the HealthWorks® employee assistance program in Eau Claire, Wisconsin, says, "In general, I would encourage supervisors to respond compassionately to an employee that approaches them with personal problems. Supervisors need to recognize that many employees have personal situations that could eventually affect their job performance." But, she adds, "while supervisors can be supportive, they need to maintain a clear boundary between the counselor and supervisory role. That's why EAPs can be so effective."

As companies increasingly focus on work/life issues, it is more common for managers to acknowledge the impact of an employee's personal life on job performance. In addition, strong relationships frequently develop between managers and subordinates, and those relationships can be a very positive and motivating force. Certainly managers are human and often feel compassion for employees who are experiencing difficult issues, but it is not appropriate to become personally involved in helping an employee work through these issues.

"Employers cite the supervisor's ability to focus on job performance and refer employees with personal problems to EAP professionals as the most valuable benefit of having an employee assistance program," Pierzina says.

That focus on performance is key. The problem isn't that Joan's husband is suffering from a terminal illness. The problem is that Joan's performance has been declining. While managers can, and should, express compassion for their employees, they must maintain their focus on performance issues. Pierzina offers the following dos and don'ts for dealing with these sensitive issues:

➤ Don't make value judgments about the employee; just focus on work performance.

➤ Do pick a private meeting place and allow ample time for discussion.

➤ Don't diagnose or label the employee. Your focus is work performance, not the employee's mental health.

➤ Do base your comments on job performance criteria.

➤ Don't allow employees to use you as a counselor.

➤ Do be consistent in expectations of performance for all employees.

- ▶ Don't discuss personal problems unless they occur on the job.
- ▶ Do be supportive.

While managers can and should encourage employees to take advantage of EAP services when available, the use of these services should be voluntary. However, while an employee may exercise his or her right to not use these services, the employee must be prepared to face the consequences of continued poor or inappropriate performance triggered by whatever personal issues that employee is facing.

CONCLUSION

What does it take to motivate today's employees?

Little things. Simple things.

It takes commitment. Regardless of the economy, regardless of unemployment statistics, it is always in a company's best interest to attract and retain good employees. Recognizing this and being committed to taking action to ensure that good employees aren't lost to competitors is the first step toward building a motivated workforce.

It takes an understanding of the needs and desires of today's diverse workforce. Each employee is different. Each employee will react differently to various motivators. Managers who are committed to motivating employees must take the time to understand their staff's interests, needs, and goals.

It takes clear direction and consistent feedback. Starting from the premise that all employees want to do a good job, managers need to work with employees to establish expectations, to show them how their daily activities impact the department and the organization, and to provide feedback (and course correction!) as necessary.

It takes communication. Employees need to be kept informed about issues that impact their jobs — and they need to be provided with ample opportunities to share ideas and provide feedback.

It takes recognition. Too many employees are starved for simple acknowledgement of their hard work. Managers have the power to provide that feedback in large and small ways on a regular basis. "Good job." "Thank you." It's not difficult. It doesn't take a lot of time. But the impact of recognition — even simple recognition — can be tremendous.

The challenge of motivating employees is universal, affecting businesses large and small. It is a challenge that will continue into the future as the population ages and companies seek capable, motivated replacements to fill the widening talent gap.

OTHER TITLES IN THE SELF-COUNSEL SERIES

**The HR Book:
Human Resources
Management for
Small Business**

Lin Grensing-Pophal
1-55180-241-4
$21.95 US/CDN

Finding and keeping good employees is
crucial to the efficient operation and success
of every business. From hiring and orientation to developing company policies and
negotiating employment contracts, today's
employers have the opportunity to select and
nurture the employees who most closely fit
their company's culture and performance
objectives.

The HR Book contains checklists and
completed samples of all the forms necessary
to maintain a streamlined, productive work
force. This book covers all the essentials of
human resource management:

- Preparing for hiring
- Knowing the law
- Developing interview and questioning
  skills
- Selecting your candidate
- Starting employees on the right track
- Conducting performance evaluations
- Maintaining a fully functioning work
  force

**Telecommuting:
Managing Off-Site
Staff for Small Business**

Lin Grensing-Pophal
1-55180-308-9
$16.95 US/$20.95 CDN

Does your business need more employees
but you don't have the office space to accommodate them? Does someone on your staff
want to work from home? Do you want to
promote a flexible work environment, but
fear losing profits? Telecommuting may be
the answer.

The changing face of today's workforce
and workplace means that employers need to
seek alternative solutions to accommodating
the needs of workers and expanding their
businesses. *Telecommuting: Managing Off-Site
Staff for Small Business* provides managers
with the tools to set up and maintain a productive telecommuting program that benefits
both employees and employers.

This book includes information on:

- Determining whether teleworking is
  right for your company
- Assessing current and new teleworking
  candidates
- Training telemanagers and teleworkers
- Communicating effectively
- Setting up the home office

ORDER FORM

All prices are subject to change without notice. Books are available in book, department, and stationery stores. If you cannot buy the book through a store, please use this order form, or visit our Web site at <www.self-counsel.com>.

Name _____

Address _____

Charge to ❏ Visa   ❏ MasterCard

Account number _____

Validation date _____

Expiry date _____

Signature _____

Shipping and handling charges will apply.

In Canada, 7% GST will be added.

In Washington, 7.8% sales tax will be added.

YES, please send me:

_____   *The HR Book*

_____   *Telecommuting*

❏ Check here for a free catalog.

In the USA
Please send your order to:
Self-Counsel Press
1704 N. State Street
Bellingham, WA 98225

In Canada
Please send your order to the nearest location:
Self-Counsel Press
1481 Charlotte Road
North Vancouver, BC V7J 1H1

Self-Counsel Press
4 Bram Court
Brampton, ON L6W 3R6

Visit our Web site at <www.self-counsel.com>.